Taking Off

Equestrian Romance Series – Book 3

Laurie Berglie

Taking Off
Copyright © 2019 Laurie Berglie
All rights reserved

ISBN: 9781692568931
Imprint: Independently published

Cover Photo Credit: Shannon Brinkman Photo

Cover Design Credit: La Familia Media

Cover Feature: Courtney Sendak of Defying Gravity Eventing riding DGE Themanintheglass (aka Riley)

To my mother, Kay Yeager – who gave me the greatest gift of all, a love of and passion for horses – and all creatures – great and small.

Chapter 1

It was late afternoon when Macy pulled into her driveway, pulled down past her house, and parked back by the barn. Early September meant summer hadn't relinquished its humid grip on Monkton, Maryland, and Macy couldn't wait for those first few cool mornings to come. She was ready to say goodbye to the heat.

As she got out of her truck, she placed a ball cap over her curly blond mane and pulled it low over her eyes to shield them from the sun. She looked out over the field, counting horse heads like she usually did. One, two, three – all accounted for. It was then that she noticed Erin leaning against the fence watching the horses. She was shadowed by a large oak tree with her shoulders sagging and head hanging, defeated. Knowing that her friend had had a tough day, Macy walked over.

"How did it go?" She asked tentatively. Erin was a private person when it came to her emotions, and the last thing Macy wanted to do was intrude. But not only was Erin her roommate, she was one of her best friends.

"Oh, you know, just about as traumatic as it could have been." Erin said with a sigh as she turned around. While she wasn't crying at the moment, Macy could tell that she had been. She went over and put her arms around her friend, bringing her into a tight embrace.

"Do you want to talk about it?"

"There's not too much to tell, honestly. We signed the papers. It's done. I'm officially divorced." At that Erin burst into tears again, and Macy pulled her back into another hug.

She sobbed for another minute before she was able to regain her composure. "It's just so sad. The whole thing. We were cordial in front of the attorneys, signed everything – it was cut and dry. I mean, I'm a family law attorney myself. I know how this goes. But then Kevin said he wanted to walk me out. When we got to my car he started to cry, so then of course I burst into tears, and we just stood there crying and holding each other." She wiped her eyes and took a deep breath. "He asked me if there was any chance I'd changed my mind. If there was any way I could give him just one baby…that this wasn't how he'd wanted things to end. But I said no, that nothing had changed. And now…now I'm a divorcee. How did this happen, Mace?"

Macy knew that her friend hadn't truly come to terms with her failed marriage, and by the looks of it, everything was suddenly hitting Erin like a ton of bricks.

Less than a year ago, just after Christmas, Erin had called and asked if she could move in with Macy for a while. She and Kevin had been fighting for quite some time, and even after counseling, they weren't making much progress. Kevin wanted a family; Erin did not. There's no real compromise in that situation.

Macy, having just lost her mother in a car accident, was happy to have some company. As the months went on, Erin seemed to take everything in stride, but today had been one for the books, and everything suddenly seemed very real.

Erin turned back around and leaned on the fence again. Even in the worst of times, when the world was spinning out of control and life had really got you down, there was something soothing about watching horses graze. Horses are the cure for just about anything.

Macy walked up beside Erin and leaned on the fence as well. Both girls laughed softly as Jazzy, the only mare in the herd, decided Fitz, Macy's young Thoroughbred, was too close to her royal highness. She let out a small squeal as she snaked her head out to try and bite the dappled grey gelding.

"What a little bitch," Erin said with a smile. Erin was a mare person through and through, and she and Jazzy were becoming quite the team. She had gotten Jazzy right off the track this past January and they were gradually working towards their goal of becoming serious eventers. Erin had started the mare over fences earlier in the summer, and Jazzy had taken to them like a fish does to water.

"She loves bossing them around," Macy said. "And the boys let her do it. I think Hunter's really in charge, but he lets Jazzy think she is. And Fitz is too afraid of her to do anything else but listen."

Hunter was Macy's older, semi-retired Warmblood. He and Macy had been stars in the dressage world back in the day – before college and life in general had gotten in the way. He had been her constant companion and saving grace when she was in vet school and working in Kentucky. Macy then acquired Fitz on a spur of the moment deal last year right before she moved back to Maryland for good. He was injured at the time and had just retired from racing. Now, over a year since that injury, he was completely rehabbed and as good as new. Macy was bringing him back into shape little by little, although she still wasn't completely sure what she wanted to do with him. She was leaning toward hunters, and of course foxhunting if he had the mind for it.

"Up for a ride?" Macy asked, hoping the ride would be a much-needed distraction for her friend.

"Absolutely. Let's go in and change."

A half hour later they were astride Jazzy and Fitz and were trotting around the perimeter of the farm. Macy's dog, Mint Julep, a Jack Russell mix, bounded along beside them. She was turning into a great little trail dog. She was excitable, of course, but always gave the horses plenty of space. The last thing Macy wanted was for her little darling to get kicked.

The two Thoroughbreds, happy to be out, matched each other stride for stride. They were quite the pair and could get competitive with each other at times. This was the only time Fitz asserted himself in any way – Jazzy ruled the roost otherwise.

"Do you have any shows lined up for the fall?" Asked Macy. Erin had taken Jazzy out a handful of times already, and the mare had handled everything remarkably well. At first, she definitely thought she was off to the races, but she quickly realized that her job had changed. Erin had taken her to a dressage schooling show; that had been Jazzy's first show and thus a learning experience. Then she had taken her to the Thoroughbreds-only show hosted by the Mid-Atlantic Horse Rescue. It was there that Jazzy seemed to put two and two together and exceled. She had come home Champion Cross Rail Jumper. Baby steps for the greenie.

"I think I'm taking her to the CT at Olney at the end of the month. That will be a great intro for her into the wonderful world of eventing," she smiled. "Dressage first and then the show jumping – it will be nice and laidback too. You should bring Fitz. I know you haven't started jumping him yet, but you could just do a dressage test."

"You know, I think I might. Will Molly bring Gypsy?"

"She's planning on it. We'll both be competing in Elementary."

"Uh oh. Sister versus sister! Who will I root for?" Macy laughed. Molly, Erin's sister, had been her best friend since elementary school. Two years ago, Molly had come to Kentucky to stay with Macy for the summer.

Since Molly was a writer, she could work from anywhere, but it was there that she met Beau Bridges, who also happened to be Macy's colleague. Molly and Beau were a match made in heaven, and they recently celebrated their one year wedding anniversary. They lived a few miles down the street, and Molly kept her mare at her parents' farm, which was just a few minutes down the road in the other direction.

"You'd better root for me!" Erin joked. "I know Molly's your BFF and all, but I'm your roommate. Besides, Jazzy will beat up Fitz if you don't."

"Ha – Jazzy will beat up Fitz regardless." The two laughed as they gathered their reins and asked for the canter.

After a few minutes at the brisk pace, they pulled up the horses, brought them back to a walk, and Erin gave a big sigh. "Thanks for this. I needed to get my mind off of everything. Poor Jazzy, she's all I have now. I'm going to throw everything I have into her training. She won't know what to do with me."

"I think she'll enjoy every second. That girl is a work horse. You two are going to be a force to be reckoned with once you really get started."

"I can't wait. Of course, we'll take it step by step, but I'm already dreaming of Fair Hill!"   "You'll get there soon enough; I can promise you that."

"In the meantime, I'm going to check the calendar and try to plan at least one show or something once a month. Even if it's just schooling off-site somewhere. I'd like to go out to Loch Moy soon too. Their cross derbies look so fun, don't they?"

"They do! I bet Molly would love to do one too." Molly, who had a background mostly in the hunters, was planning on eventing for the first time. It was going to be fun watching both sisters bring their horse kids along.

"I'll tag along if you just go to school, but of course I can't do anything until I start getting this kid over some fences." She patted Fitz's glossy neck. He was definitely healed enough to start doing small cross-rails.

"Well I guess we'd better head back. I need to call my parents and Molly; I know they'll want to see how everything went today. I hope I don't start crying again."

"It's okay if you do. Don't be so hard on yourself."

"Thanks, I know I shouldn't be. But I guess since this is what I do for a living, I feel like I should have handled it a bit better, almost like I should be immune to it. Oh well – you live and you learn, right?"

"Right. And now you're onto bigger and better adventures!"

Chapter 2

Later that night Erin laid in her bed, book in hands, trying to concentrate on the words before her. After reading the same page over and over, she gave up and let her thoughts overtake her.

Her mom and Molly hadn't waited for Erin to call them. They were waiting at the barn when she and Macy rode up. Erin was proud of herself – she only broke down in tears once. Other than that, she was able to describe the day to her mom and sister, and she had to admit that she had felt better afterwards. Maybe each time she talked about it, it would get easier and easier until one day she could recount her divorce in the same manner in which she ordered her coffee or chatted with a client. Like a regular everyday occurrence.

One day.

One day, it would get easier. She kept having to remind herself that the hard part was indeed over. The hard part had been living with Kevin, the constant fighting and back and forth, the disappointment in his eyes when he looked at her.

Did she feel guilty? Yes, a little. Before they had gotten married, they'd had 'the kid talk.' Kevin was adamant – yes, he absolutely wanted kids someday. And Erin, well, she *guessed* she'd want them too. *Some day.* She'd never been someone who liked kids. When she was a teenager, neighbors and family friends had asked if she'd babysit for them, and she shied away from those opportunities as fast as she could. (Thank goodness Molly always jumped to the rescue on that front).

When a cousin or other relative had a new baby, she never asked to hold him or her. Kids just weren't on her radar – it was always just about horses. And then as she got older, it was about horses and her job.

She figured that she'd love her own children, of course, and that someday she'd be ready to have them. So yes, Kevin entered into the marriage thinking that at some point they'd start a family together.

But as another year came and went and she was still no closer to wanting kids – farther away, actually – Kevin got worried. When can we start trying, he'd ask? Maybe next year, she'd say. And so it went.

Until Kevin finally gave her an ultimatum. They were in their thirties now, so it was a baby, or he was going to walk. And while Erin didn't actually believe that it would come to this, that he'd really divorce her over a baby who didn't even exist, she also didn't blame him. She was the one who had changed her mind. She went back on her word, essentially.

They were twenty-four when they got married. They were babies themselves – what did they know? How was she supposed to know that the older she got, the more she felt she wasn't meant to be a mother? She couldn't see into the future. She couldn't predict how she'd grow and change and feel about certain things.

But – at the end of the day – she had gone back on a promise. She had told Kevin, point blank, that yes, she'd have his kids one day. And when that day came, she just couldn't go through with it. Nor could she explain why. She just didn't want to be a mom. And here she was, nine years later and alone.

People told her she was selfish. Only selfish people don't want kids, they'd snarl. But isn't wanting kids a selfish act too? The desire to have something is just the same as the desire to *not have* something. But since the majority of society reside on the side of having kids, that's the norm, the rule. And Erin was the exception.

She had begged and pleaded with Kevin – wasn't she enough? The two of them had had such a wonderful marriage until things went south. They had been so good together – similar likes and dislikes. They agreed on where they wanted to live and how they wanted to grow old together. They had the same outlook on life and love, religion and politics – all those big ticket items. Except children.

One thing. It was just one thing. But, unfortunately, it was a big one and it drove a wedge in between them. Counseling didn't help as there was really no way to compromise on this one. You couldn't have half a kid. Someone had to win, and someone had to lose. Or, each could go their separate ways.

Erin, as an attorney, never thought she'd be on the other side of that table. The one holding back tears, signing paper after paper, ending the only thing she had ever felt sure of. Feeling like a complete and utter failure.

On the verge of tears again, Erin got up and went into the bathroom where she filled a glass with water. After she drank it, she walked across the hall and knocked on Macy's door. As Macy opened it, Erin bent down to scoop up Julep, who was getting ready to jump all over Erin anyway.

"I need Julep tonight. I'm sure you understand." She said with a sad smile as she held the dog close to her chest and turned back to her room.

Chapter 3

Erin sat at her desk in her office trying to concentrate on the mountain of work spread before her. It had been exactly one week since her divorce had been finalized, and she was having trouble shaking off the gloom she'd felt since that afternoon. She swiveled her chair to face the floor-to-ceiling windows behind her. The view of Baltimore City from this high-rise displayed a beautiful, late summer day. The humidity had finally broken, and the temps were hovering in the upper-seventies. Erin longed to be with Jazzy. She longed to be anywhere but here.

"Knock, knock," came a voice at her door. It was her secretary, Robyn, and she was holding an envelope in her hands. "Courier just dropped this off. I think it's about the Madison-Richards case." That case was turning out to be a nightmare.

Erin held out her hand. "Great, thank you."

"How are you doing?" Robyn asked, concern in her eyes. She was in her mid-fifties and had known Erin since she had started with the firm right out of law school.

"Honestly, terrible. I hardly batted an eyelash when we separated. I packed up and moved out and felt in my heart that we were over. I was hurt, of course, but now…I guess the finality of it just feels like such a punch in the gut."

"Maybe you felt like he would change his mind?"

"Maybe. I don't think so though. I was beginning to envision my future, and I wasn't including him in it. I felt like I was moving on, but maybe on some level I did think he was going to drop everything and ask to start over."

She looked down at her desk and pointed to the envelope Robyn had just handed her. "I guess I should be grateful that it was amicable. I don't think I could have handled it had it turned into a knockdown, drag out fight like this one."

"That is something to be thankful for. We've sure seen some ugly ones, haven't we?"

"We have indeed. Actually, mine might have been one of the easiest ever. We rented our apartment, so it's not like we owned a house together. We didn't have any kids to share custody of, obviously. He took his car, and I took mine. We split our assets in our savings account evenly. Except for my clothes and some personal belongings, I didn't want any of the furniture. The room Macy rents me is furnished, and Kevin is still in the apartment. I'm back in Monkton where I started. It's almost like the marriage didn't even happen." With that, tears began to glisten in Erin's eyes.

"Sweetheart, don't say that. I know it's so hard, but like you tell your clients, everything happens for a reason, and each day will get better and better. Why don't you leave early and go ride that pretty horse of yours? You only have one other appointment this afternoon, and I can reschedule it if you'd like."

"You're right. I think I will leave now. Being outside with the horses is the best medicine." She grabbed her briefcase and put her laptop inside along with the info regarding the Madison-Richards case. "I'll review this later," she said with a smirk and an eyeroll.

"Enjoy the fresh air. See you tomorrow."

As Erin merged north onto I-83, she took a deep, lung-filling breath of air. She was so grateful for friends and people like Robyn in her life. But there had to be more than this. There had to be more than sitting in rush hour traffic twice a day, being cooped up in an office smaller than your average-sized horse stall and dealing with couples who want to rip each other's throats out.

At one point in her career, Erin thrived on the drama. She was known for her ferocity in the courtroom and her ability to win cases initially thought doomed. But now, it was getting old and she was getting jaded. Truthfully, it had started taking its toll on her even before she and Kevin separated. Going to work every single day and dealing with what amounted to constant hatred had gotten to her.

In law school, her professors had told her that family law was one of the most difficult and that many attorneys switched specialties not long after. But she felt pulled in that direction, so she went full steam ahead.

But now, she was done. There's got to be something more.

For the time being though, she'd try to concentrate on the here and now, and take her own advice to take everything one day at a time. And today was a gorgeous day. The sun was shining, there was a warm breeze blowing, and it was only two o'clock in the afternoon. She had the windows rolled down, her hair was pulled back in a ponytail, and she was ready to shed her business suit for her breeches and boots.

But first, coffee! Erin took the Shawan Road exit off of I-83 and stopped at the Starbucks on York Road before heading north to Macy's farm.

"Treat yo'self, as they say," she said to herself as she pulled up to the drive-thru to place her order.

Minutes later and with an iced white chocolate mocha in the cup holder, she motored towards home. Using her Bluetooth, she called Macy.

"Hey Erin, what's up?" Macy asked when she

answered.

"Hey! I'm on my way home and wondered if you were free to go riding in about an hour or so."

"Actually, yes. I'm in White Hall right now about to drop off some meds to a client, but then I'm done."

"Great! I'll see you at home in a bit."

An hour later dressed in her Tredstep schooling breeches and fully-caffeinated thanks to Starbucks, Erin strode into the tack room to find Macy already there and pulling Hunter's tack off the rack.

"I figured I'd take the old guy out today. I haven't ridden him in at least a week."

"Perfect. I know he likes getting out too."

The two girls pulled all three horses inside; Macy was going to leave Fitz in his stall with a flake of hay so he wouldn't be too distraught at being left behind.

"How come you left early today?" Macy asked while currying the dirt off Hunter's chestnut coat.

Erin looked up from brushing Jazzy's tail and sighed. "Honestly, I just couldn't take it anymore. If I had to sit there another minute, I was going to spontaneously combust."

"I remember that feeling. The last time I combusted, I quit my job on the spot and ended up back in Maryland with Fitz in tow." She gave a small laugh. "I was so upset at myself then, but now that some time has passed and I have a little perspective, I've learned that it's okay to combust every so often. I have learned to give myself a little grace."

It had been just over a year since Macy's mom, Hadley, had tragically passed away from a car accident, and Macy was finally feeling like herself again. Her world had been turned upside down, but thanks to her friends, her brother and his family, and her boyfriend, Adam, she had come out on the other side better than ever. But it had been touch and go there for a while.

"I was looking out the window and daydreaming when Robyn walked in with paperwork for this huge case I'm working on…and I just thought, I'm going to take that file, set it on fire, walk out of here, and never look back."

"I would imagine things are just hitting a bit too close to home right now."

"They are, but if I'm honest with myself, I've been unhappy there for a few years now. And not at that particular firm per se, but with family law. It's so draining."

"So, what are you going to do?" Macy asked as she smoothed a pad over Hunter's back and reached for his saddle.

"Well, I don't think I should make any rash decisions…but I don't know. I feel like I need to make some changes, and soon. But I want to be sure about everything – I don't just want this to be the divorce talking."

"Good idea. But I will say, follow your gut. If your gut says you're done with family law, or if you just need an extended break, listen to it and take a break."

"I imagine this is also how Molly felt, to some degree, when she left home and moved in with you for the summer two years ago."

"Exactly. And look how that worked out for her?" Molly had met Beau, fallen in love, and written her best-selling novel to date during that summer in Lexington.

"So, you're saying I need to get 'back to basics,' huh?" Erin laughed as that was what Macy had called Molly's trip.

"Yes! Sometimes you just have to slow things

down," Macy said with a smile. She had loved that summer with Molly. Just two best friends, living together, being young and carefree. "If you could do anything right now, what would it be?"

Erin thought for a moment as she tightened Jazzy's girth. The red mare pinned her ears and snarled her nose, but her bark was worse than her bite. She was all talk.

"If I could do anything, I'd quit my job and try and make a living with horses. Maybe take retirees off the track, retrain them as sporthorses, and sell them. Or maybe start a lesson and training barn. Horses all day, every day. Wouldn't that be nice?"

Macy, as a vet whose days actually did revolve around horses, whole-heartedly agreed. "Some days are tough, as you know, but there's a reason why I chose a profession where my colleagues have four legs instead of two."

They led their horses outside to the mounting block, rolled down their stirrups, and checked their girths one final time.

After they mounted, Erin turned Jazzy towards the back of the property and the two girls walked side-by-side along the fence-line.

"You know, while we're on this subject, there is one thing I've always regretted," said Erin. "When I was just out of college, before I started law school, I applied to be a working student for a variety of eventing professionals in the area. Most were in Maryland, Pennsylvania, and Virginia, and two of them accepted me, Amanda Michaels and Ian O'Ryan. I had to send in a video of me riding and showing, all that stuff. My thought was to take a year off before law school, do the working student thing, learn from the pros, and compete as much as possible. But I ended up turning both down and going straight to law school. At the time, I thought that was the most grown up thing to do." She made a gagging noise and stuck her tongue out.

"I had no idea you had wanted to be a working student. It's a shame you hadn't taken one. Who knows what would have happened? That could have changed the trajectory of your entire life."

"Right? I think about it way too often. Definitely my biggest regret."

"Why don't you do it now?"

"Mace, that was more than ten years ago. I'm thirty-three now. I feel like the window to be a working student has come and gone."

"It absolutely hasn't. Besides, no harm in putting some feelers out. Maybe you need to recapture that year now. Take a leave of absence from work and live that lost year." Macy looked over at Erin. "I'm completely serious. I think it's high-time you spontaneously combusted!"

"Maybe you're right," Erin smiled over at her friend. And at that, they heeled their horses into a canter and took off into the gleaming countryside.

Chapter 4

Olney Farm in Joppa is the quintessential Maryland horse farm. Established in 1855, it has remained in the same family since, and its lush pastures and rolling hills are home to horses and Shetland ponies alike. Turning into their treelined drive is like taking a step back in time. It's stunningly bucolic.

These were some of Erin's thoughts as she walked over to watch Macy and Fitz warm up. She, Macy, and Molly were competing in a combined training event, so it was a big day for the three girls. And to top it all off, it was Fitz's very first show. Since the two weren't jumping regularly, Macy was only doing the Intro C dressage test.

"How's he doing?" Erin asked as she watched Macy trot Fitz around a large grass paddock that was being used as a warm-up area.

"Cool as a cucumber. I, on the other hand, am nervous and am sweating like a pig." Macy grinned as she trotted a perfect figure eight. She and Fitz were set to go on in about fifteen minutes.

Molly walked up behind Erin and spoke directly to her. "They look good, don't they? You'd never know this was Fitz's first show." Fitz, dappled grey coat gleaming and ebony mane and tail sparkling, looked terrific. He bounded around effortlessly, and while he was aware of his surroundings, he was still focused on Macy's instructions.

"She was smart to take him off the farm to school with us this summer. He looks phenomenal. Thank goodness she rescued him from his previous owner. If she hadn't been there to take ownership, he would have been put to sleep."

"I get so upset just thinking about it. But it was meant to be. She was meant to save his life and come home to us." Molly smiled over at Erin. A lot had happened to the three of them in the last two years, some good, some bad, but through it all they just grew closer.

After a few more circles at the trot, Macy slowed Fitz down to the walk. "Time check?" She called over.

"You go on in eight minutes," Erin called back.

"Okay, let's head over there."

The dressage ring was just on the other side of the driveway from where she had been warming up. Molly walked over to the ring steward to check Macy in while Erin handed Macy a bottle of water.

"You're all set," Molly said as she walked over. "You're after the rider who just entered. Also, mom says good luck. She's back at the trailer watching the horses."

"Thanks! I'm so excited but also scared – I don't think I've made it into the show ring since vet school."

"That explains why you're so nervous," Erin said. "But as soon as you get in there, it will all come back to you, and you'll clean up! Do you remember your test? Want me to run you through it again?"

"No, if I think about it anymore, I'll just confuse myself. We're at the point of no return!"

The steward called over to Macy that she could prepare to enter the ring. Erin and Molly called their good luck wishes and walked to the side of the ring where chairs were set up for spectators. Both pulled out their phones. Erin was going to take video while Molly would snap a bunch of photos.

From the moment Macy trotted down centerline to salute the judge, the girls knew their friend had it in the bag. Macy's test was virtually flawless with Fitz, head completely in the game, listening to her every command.

"I'd say we're witnessing the beginning of a

fabulous new team," Molly whispered to Erin. Both girls were grinning ear-to-ear as they watched their friend perform the various movements around the ring. They could also see the smile grow on Macy's face as she got towards the end of the test. She knew her horse was doing a great job and that they were almost finished. Before she knew it, they were floating back down centerline for the final salute to the judge, and she could hear Erin and Molly whooping for her on the sidelines.

"He's stunning," said the judge as Macy approached. "Absolutely beautiful test."

"Thank you," Macy answered shyly. "It's his first show."

"Really? Well I'd say you have a star on your hands. Well done."

Almost two hours later, Erin and Molly found themselves in the same warm-up area putting Jazzy and Gypsy through their paces. Both girls had their hands full. Neither mare was out of control; they were both just excited as young OTTBs almost always were. When asked to canter, Gypsy crow-hopped a tad; Jazzy let out a squeal followed by a mild buck.

"Woo!" Called out Erin who was grinning ear-to-ear. "These girls are feeling it today!" A few spirited bucks and kicks didn't faze Erin one bit. She had spent her whole life riding Thoroughbreds, and she loved their fire.

Molly wasn't really bothered either, but her tight smile gave her slight nerves away. "I think we're about to put in some very entertaining tests!"

Macy had volunteered to stay back at the trailer with Fitz, so Karen was on hand to watch and help assist her daughters.

"I love seeing you two back in the show ring together," she said with a smile. "Although I see our fillies are full of themselves today." Karen, an experienced horsewoman herself, was also used to these antics.

"Mom, what time is it?" Molly asked. She was first in the ring. Then there was another competitor in between her and Erin.

"It's almost one o'clock. You go on in nine minutes."

"Okay, let's head over to the ring then."

"I'm going to do one more canter transition with Jazzy, then I'll be right there to root you on.

Despite both mares' silly behavior during warm-up, they settled once in the dressage ring and put in respectable performances. Erin came out of the ring beaming and high-fived her sister who had waited to watch.

"I think your scores will be close," said Karen as she handed a water bottle to Erin. "Jazzy seemed a bit more forward, which is what judges want to see, but Gypsy's canter transitions were spot-on. Good job girls." Karen had long since given up competing and instead enjoyed the role of horse show mom.

When they arrived back to the trailer, they saw a blue ribbon hanging on the door of the dressing room and Macy looking incredibly pleased with herself.

"I knew you guys would take first – well done!" Cried Erin.

"Thanks! I mean, it's only Intro, but I can't help but be happy. He put in a great effort. Who knows, maybe I'll catch the eventing bug myself!"

"Erin, Molly, you two have about twenty minutes before stadium jumping. You should probably take some warm-up jumps now," said Karen, pointing in the direction of the grass ring where they'd finish the day.

As competitors in Elementary, they were only jumping two foot fences. They each took turns warming up over the few cross-rails and verticals set up just outside the main ring, both trotting and cantering over each. The horses had settled beautifully and took the jumps like old pros.

Like an event, this phase was judged on faults for knocking down a rail, or refusing a jump, as well as an optimum time. If you went over that time, you'd receive penalty faults. Molly was first into the ring.

She trotted Gypsy in a circle at the top, then heeled her into a canter towards her first fence. There were a variety of brightly-painted verticals and oxers, but nothing too spooky or distracting; it was the perfect course for a young horse new to the world of competition.

Molly's strategy was to take it slow and easy. She was after a clear and careful round, and if that meant she was over the optimum time, then so be it. It was more important for Gypsy to have a good experience, be patient, and learn to listen to her rider. The last thing Molly wanted was to rush around the course, teaching Gypsy at such an impressionable age that it's okay to rush the fences. As she matured, she would learn the name of the game, but for now, a steady round was a safe round.

And that's what they ended up with, a clean round but with a few time faults for going over the optimum time.

"You two looked like show hunters out there!" Laughed Erin. She, too, was taking a similar approach – slow and steady – but Jazzy was naturally more forward than Gypsy.

Molly had competed seriously in the hunters for

years, so that was a compliment. "If we don't make it as eventers, then I guess we have a Plan B."

Karen walked over and gave Gypsy a well-deserved pat. "Your form is impeccable Molly. Just beautiful."

Erin's round was almost a carbon copy of Molly's but quite a bit faster. Jazzy didn't exactly rush the fences per se, but she was definitely a girl on the move. But Erin was strong and able to bring her back when the horse got a little antsy on the approach. All-in-all, it was a round to be proud of.

When they got back to the trailer, Macy had good news. "One of my clients is here with her horse today too and just came by to tell me your dressage results. Molly, you got third, and Erin, you were fourth! What a great day for us!"

The two sisters high-fived yet again, then dismounted and began to untack and cool out their horses.

At the end of the day, Erin came in first in the stadium jumping with no faults at all. Molly was fourth with six time faults. Because the scores from dressage and stadium jumping were combined together, Erin ended the day with a red second place ribbon, and Molly proudly displayed her white fourth place ribbon on Gypsy's bridle. Macy was over the moon with Fitz's blue ribbon and couldn't wait to compete in the stadium jumping phase the next time out.

Chapter 5

Erin climbed into her bed later that night after the show grateful to be off her feet. As far as she was concerned, horse shows were the very best way to spend a day, but they sure were exhausting. Karen had driven her four horse trailer and since Gypsy lived at her farm, they dropped Erin and Macy's horses off first before going home.

Macy had worried that Hunter would be upset to be left completely alone, but the old gelding could not have cared less. He gave his friends the briefest glance as they loaded onto the trailer that morning and then turned back to grazing on the still-green early autumn grass as if nothing was amiss.

Jazzy and Fitz, on the other hand, were excited to see their friend when they returned home, galloping way into the field to see Hunter and tell him all about their day. Or, at least that's what Erin and Macy imagined they were doing. In all actuality, they probably just wanted to make sure Hunter had saved them some grass!

Now in bed, Erin smiled over at the red ribbon lying on her nightstand. She was so excited for her future with Jazzy. The mare was proving to be a willing partner, and Erin was sure she would love eventing. She had handled her transition out of racing and into a second career in stride, and Erin was proud of her fur-kid. After today's successful show, she was thinking a little light cross country schooling at Tranquillity Manor was in order. She would treat it more like a trail ride, just a nice hack out in the fields. She didn't want to over-face the mare by introducing too much too soon but popping over a few small logs out in the field would be the perfect place to start.

Even though her body was exhausted, Erin felt keyed up all of a sudden, so she grabbed her phone and started scrolling through social media. It had been a while since she had checked Facebook – months, probably – and her heart caught in her throat when she pulled up her profile.

Erin Peters.

She had kept her last name, Sorrenson, for work purposes, but she had taken her husband's name legally. Mr. and Mrs. Kevin Peters. Those people no longer exist, she thought sadly. She had already begun the process of changing her name back to Sorrenson, so she may as well change it on Facebook now. But then the world would know. It would be Facebook-official that her marriage had failed.

Maybe she should just delete her account altogether?

After going back and forth for a few moments, she decided that this was Future Erin's Problem, as she liked to call it, and put her phone away completely. But just as she sat it down, it buzzed with a text message from Molly.

M: Hi! Good job today! Mom wants to know what you'd like to do for your birthday. It's next week in case you forgot lol

E: Good job yourself! We have some great ponies! Omg...the big 3-4. I'm not ready for this.

M: Well we're celebrating, like it or not. ;) Do you want a family dinner in, or do you want to go out to a restaurant?

E: Definitely in. The less people I'm around, the better.

M: I figured that. Mom wants to host, but I told her I'd bake the cake.

E: That sounds perfect – thanks!

M: Great! I'll text Macy about it too. Anyone else you'd like

me to invite? Adam?
E: Sure, Adam too. Thanks sis!

The sisters texted back and forth a bit more before saying goodnight. Molly, too, was tired from the long day of showing.

Still relatively awake though, Erin turned on the tv and flipped channels. She stopped on a rerun of one of her favorite shows, "The Office." Actually, it had been Kevin's all-time favorite, and he had always said she was the Pam to his Jim. A sadness suddenly swept over Erin, and she had the overwhelming urge to text Kevin.

But what would I even say?

Stop it, she told herself. Communicating with him in any way really wouldn't do either of them any good. They were over. They had made their choices.

To satisfy her curiosity, Erin logged into Facebook again and pulled up Kevin's profile. They were still friends, so she was able to see his entire page. She gave a soft cry when she saw that Kevin had made some updates, the first to his profile picture. The one that had been there since they had separated, of just him swinging a golf club, had been replaced. Now pictured was Kevin with his arm around another girl, both smiling broadly at the camera.

Next, he had changed his relationship status. After they had separated, he had hidden that section so it didn't say anything either way. Now it read, In a Relationship with Delaney Stevens. A quick click on her name took Erin to Delaney's profile. It was private, of course, but Erin was able to look at a few older cover photos. Delaney was stunning. Blond, tan, blue-eyed. She looked like she belonged on the Southern California coast, not here in Maryland.

As tears began to stream down Erin's cheeks, she

clicked back over to Kevin's profile where she unfriended him. She couldn't bear to see updates of his newfound love pop up in her feed.

And with that, she hopped out of bed and knocked on Macy's door. When Macy opened it and saw the tears in Erin's eyes, she said, "Julep?"

"Yes," answered Erin, holding her arms out. "It's another one of those nights. Thank you," she said as Macy handed over the little dog who started wildly kissing Erin's cheeks.

Dogs always made everything better.

Chapter 6

"I have Ms. Martin on line one," Robyn said over the phone.

"Oh good, put her through." The call clicked over. "Alexa!" Alexa Martin was Erin's best friend from college. They had dormed together all four years and even lived together in the city for a few years while Erin was in law school. The two girls had had some wild times together.

"Erin, hi! How are you?" Alexa trilled.

"Hanging in there. It's so good to hear your voice."

"I know, it's been way too long. But I'm sure you know why I'm calling – it's almost your birthday and you know what that means!"

Every year around Erin's birthday, she, Alexa, and a bunch of their friends got together for dinner in the city and then bar crawled through Canton or Fells Point. Erin had always looked forward to seeing her friends and having a night out on the town, but she didn't think she'd be good company right now.

She sighed into the phone. "Alexa, I don't know. I don't think I'm up to it this year."

"No way, you're not getting out of this, my dear. If there's ever been a year you *do* need this, it's this year. Besides, I've already talked to the gang, and they're all in. This Friday night. You pick the restaurant for dinner and then we'll go from there. Of course, we'll hit your favorite, James Joyce."

The James Joyce Irish Pub in Harbor East was one of Erin's favorites, but now just thinking about it made her heart ache. Years ago, she had been standing in the crowded pub, beer in hand, when a cute guy by the name of Kevin tripped over his own feet and knocked into her on his way to the bar. And the rest, as they say, is history.

"I think we can skip James Joyce this year."

"We'll do whatever you want as long as you say you're going." Alexa wasn't taking no for an answer.

"Fine. But I'm not staying out late. Dinner and one drink and then I'm on my way home. And I'm pulling my standard Irish Goodbye." Erin was known for leaving parties without saying goodbye to anyone. She always texted everyone later, and they all thought it was funny how she got away with it over and over.

"Stop acting like an old schoolmarm. You'll feel more like yourself when you get out there and get a few drinks in you. Invite Molly and Macy too."

They chatted for a few more minutes before they hung up. Alexa had moved to DC for work about two years ago, and though they kept in touch as much as possible, it hadn't been like before when they were living in the city only a few blocks from each other. It would be nice to see everyone and catch up.

Erin hadn't been able to decide on a restaurant for dinner, so the girls decided to splurge and treat the birthday girl to a steak dinner at Ruth's Chris. The five of them sat around talking and laughing, red wine glasses in hand, and reminiscing about the good old days. Now everyone was in their early to mid-thirties with spouses, demanding jobs, and children, for some. Life had changed, but their friendships had not. As they sang happy birthday to her, Erin was overwhelmed with gratitude.

"I'm sorry your sister and Macy couldn't make

it," Alexa said as they were putting their jackets on and heading out to grab some more drinks.

"Me too. Macy was still on an emergency call when I left, and Molly already had plans. But it's okay – I'm just happy to see you all." She hugged Alexa tightly.

"Uber's here," yelled Emma from just outside the restaurant. As the girls piled in, she heard Emma tell the driver to head to James Joyce.

Well here goes nothing, she thought. Hopefully she wouldn't be flooded with memories of Kevin and the many good times they'd shared there.

The pub was packed. The girls made their way to the bar where they ordered a round of shots to get things started off.

"Tequila for the birthday girl!" Alexa sang as she passed around the shot glasses. True, Erin loved her tequila.

"We need to take it slow," laughed Susanne. "We're old, remember. This is going to hurt tomorrow."

"Agreed," said Erin. "But Alexa has that gleam in her eye! We're all in trouble!"

"A toast to our favorite attorney, equestrian, and best friend," said Alexa with her glass raised. Erin was sure Alexa was already pretty drunk.

"To Erin!" They sang and down the hatch went the shot.

"Another round!" Cried Alexa.

"Oh Lord, someone stop her!"

"One more and then we're cool it for a few!" Alexa was in rare form, and before the girls knew it, five more shots were procured.

"Alexa, if I keep listening to you, I won't see 35!" Erin laughed as she took yet another shot of tequila. Back in the day, she and Alexa would have led this charge together, but she just wasn't herself right now. Erin knew it was only a matter of time before she felt better, so for now, she just followed Alexa's lead.

The girls milled around the bar and ran into others they knew. As the night wore on, more and more people spilled in, and Erin, pretty drunk, was enjoying herself.

"I see that you defriended me on Facebook. What the hell, Erin?" Asked a too-familiar voice behind her. She turned around and there was Kevin. His boyish features were accentuated in the dark light of the pub, and Erin found herself looking at him with fresh eyes. Had his eyes always been that chocolatey brown? Were his lips always so full? How had she missed those things all these years?

Stop, it's the alcohol talking, she chastised herself.

"Are you really mad?" She asked.

"I am. That was hurtful. We can still be friends, can't we?"

"Of course we can be friends, but…seeing you…moving on to your new perfect life. Well, it hurt more than I thought. I'm sorry though – it was childish."

"It's not a perfect life. I didn't want a new one. I was happy with the old one."

"But you weren't!"

"I was happy with most of it…just not all of it."

"What are you saying Kevin?"

"I'm saying I miss you. I came here tonight because I figured you'd be here. Hoped you would be anyway."

"I miss you too, but nothing has changed. I am *not* having your babies. I'm *not* having anyone's babies." She shook her head. No more shots, Alexa.

Erin could see the sadness in Kevin's eyes. It

broke her heart to hurt this man, the man who had been so good to her. Minus the kid debacle, he had been a loving husband, and she had been blissfully happy for so long. But she wasn't going to have kids just to make someone else happy.

"I know," he said. "It's okay." With that he pulled her into a hug and held her tightly. Erin allowed herself to melt into him. She fit so perfectly – she always had. Her head fell squarely on his chest as he rested his chin on top of her head. She wrapped her arms around him, and his body, his cologne – it all felt so familiar. It felt like home.

"Come back to the apartment with me," he whispered in her ear.

This is wrong. This is a mistake, she thought as they made their way back to the old apartment they'd once shared. But she couldn't help it. She was drunk and sad and lonely. And Kevin...well, he was Kevin. He was everything she knew. And, let's face it, it had been almost a year since she'd last had sex.

"Are you sure?" She asked as he laid her on the bed, their bed.

"Yes," he answered swiftly as he tugged off his shirt and unbuckled his belt. Erin took his face in her hands and pulled him to her, kissing him with everything she had. He pulled back for a moment, lifted her shirt over her head, and with one skilled flick, unsnapped the clasp of her bra.

Before Erin knew it, he was deep inside her, and she wrapped her legs around his torso as he dove farther into her, moaning along with each thrust.

The taste of his skin, the arch of his back, and firmness of his arms – it was so familiar, and yet the distance of the past year only heightened her senses to this man she had once given her whole heart to. It would be so easy to fall back into him, into this life they'd built. Having a family wouldn't be the worst thing in the world, would it? But no, she thought. She had to stay true to herself.

Kevin rolled over so Erin was on top, and she sat up and took his hands in hers, grinding up and down. Kevin knew her better than anyone else in this world, and he knew how she loved having her breasts kissed while she climaxed. He followed shortly behind, pumping into her, and she fell into his caressing arms.

The alarm clock on the nightstand read 1:03 when she awoke. Kevin was next to her, sound asleep on his back, snoring like usual. For a moment, Erin felt like she was in the twilight zone, and she had to shake her head to get her bearings. Between the alcohol and the emotional turmoil of the last few weeks, she was simply exhausted…and that exhaustion had led to this crazy behavior.

She slid out of the bed, the bed that she herself had picked out at Ethan Allen when, newly-married, they had moved into this apartment years ago, quietly grabbed her clothes, and slunk out into the living room where she quickly dressed and scheduled an uber home.

Chapter 7

Erin had hoped to sneak quietly into the house, but Julep wasn't going to let that happen. The little Jack Russel mix came bounding down the stairs, barking wildly, convinced that an intruder was breaking into her home. But as soon as she realized it was Erin, she launched into her friend's arms and replaced her loud yips with sloppy kisses.

"Erin, is that you?" Macy was walking carefully down the stairs, baseball bat in hand.

"It is, sorry to wake you. I was trying to sneak in." She noticed the bat. "Goodness, Mace, were you going to bludgeon me to death?" Erin started laughing.

"I knew you'd be in late, but Julep dashed off like it was the end of the world, so I just wanted to be safe." She leaned the bat against the hall closet. "So? How was it?"

"It was fine, fun," she said, not making eye contact.

Macy studied her friend for a moment. "What happened?"

Erin started to laugh. "I think I'm officially starting to combust. I, well...I did...a thing."

Macy held up her hand. "Wait, go no further. Come with me. I'll make some tea." She turned and headed to the kitchen. "You wreak of tequila, by the way."

"Damn Alexa..."

Erin grabbed two mugs for the tea while Macy put the kettle on. Macy then fished out some honey and tea bags from the cabinet and pulled two teaspoons from the drawer. She pointed to the table. "Sit and spill the beans."

Erin took a deep breath. "I had sex with Kevin tonight."

Macy spun quickly around, not sure she'd heard Erin correctly. "You what!?!"

"I ran into Kevin at the bar. We were all at James Joyce, and I was...well, pretty wasted. He showed up looking all cute and Kevin-y...and the next thing I know, we're back at the apartment shagging like teenagers."

"And? How do you feel?" Macy asked as she brought over the kettle and poured the steaming water.

Erin had already placed the tea bags in the mugs, and the girls both adjusted them while they steeped. "I feel weird. Like the whole thing was so strange. I was in my home, I mean my former home, and while it almost felt as if I'd never left, I also felt like an intruder."

"That makes sense. Your mark is all over...from the couches you picked out to the color of the dishtowels. But – you also haven't been there in a long time. It hasn't been your home since last year."

"Exactly. And afterwards he fell asleep, so I snuck out. I know it's not my place anymore, but it felt so odd to make off in the middle of the night." Erin started laughing. The whole scenario was just surreal.

"Do you regret it?"

Erin took a sip of her tea while she thought for a moment. "I might feel differently tomorrow, but I don't think so. In a way it was a nice reminder of how happy we were and how much I loved him. I'll always love Kevin. And the sex was great – that was never our problem," she laughed. "And hell, it's been almost a year – I was overdue."

"Do you want to get back together with him?"

"If we could go back to the way things were a few years ago, then yes. But we could never get back to that. And there are worst things in the world than starting a family with a wonderful guy like Kevin, but…I need to stick with my gut on this one. We're over."

"What if he wants you back and promises to stop asking for kids?"

"I don't think I could do it. I would want to, of course, but I know in his heart he wants a family. And I don't want to keep him from that. Nor do I want us to get back together and have him resent me years later for not giving him children."

"So tonight was like…closure?"

"Yeah, in a way I guess so. For as much as being with him felt like home, I was also acutely aware of the fact that things had changed. There is just too much water under the bridge now."

"But wait, didn't you tell me he was seeing someone?"

"Yes, he has a new girlfriend. I guess Kevin's a cheater now!"

"Does ex sex count though?" Macy asked with a wink.

"Ha! Not my problem to worry about," she smirked. She knew that Kevin wasn't the type of guy to run around. They both had been drinking and were caught up in the emotions of the night, her birthday, being at James Joyce, and the memories that will always live there.

"What will you do now? Are you going to talk to him again?"

"No, I don't think so. Boy – I'm glad my actual birthday isn't until Sunday! I have one more day to make stupid life decisions, but then I need to get it together."

"What are your goals for your new year of life?"

"I need to put some thought into that…but I think I'll be making some changes. Nothing crazy and nothing permanent. But I'm entering into a new chapter, and I'm up for a little adventure."

"Sounds like you already had one tonight!"

"I think you're right," Erin agreed as she held up her mug. "Cheers to new chapters and exciting times ahead!"

"I'll drink to that!" Macy said as they clinked mugs.

"But now it's time for bed."

Chapter 8

On Sunday the Sorrenson family, Macy and Adam included, gathered around the large dining room table at Karen and Rick's home. As usual, Karen had prepared a feast. She loved cooking, and especially loved going all out for birthdays.

"Mom, once again you've outdone yourself. This looks amazing – thank you!" Erin exclaimed as she sat down and surveyed the spread before her. All of Erin's favorites were there: a cream of crab soup appetizer, crab imperial for the entrée, baked potatoes with all the trimmings, broccoli casserole, diced carrots, corn on the cob – everything a Maryland girl loved.

"You are so welcome, my dear. We hope this is your best year yet," Karen said as she took her seat next to Rick.

"I've never had crab imperial," said Adam, who was originally from upstate New York. "I'm excited to try it."

"You'll love it," Macy grinned. "And Karen makes the best!"

The family began passing the dishes around and chatted about what they'd done over the weekend. The weather had been gorgeous, so all the girls had gone out riding, Karen included. While she didn't compete anymore, she still loved a good hack through the countryside.

"Any calls yesterday?" Macy asked Beau, Molly's husband. Beau owned Monkton Equine Medicine, and Macy had joined his practice full-time earlier that year.

"Anne Piper's mare had a mild gas colic in the

evening, but that was it. I called her this morning to check in – mare's back to normal now. But other than that, a quiet weekend."

"Good! I have a full schedule tomorrow. Business is really picking up. Any final decisions on hiring an office assistant?"

Beau had been debating on hiring an office assistant to manage some calls, paperwork, billing, sort of an admin jack of all trades.

"I think we're going to do it," he said with a smile. He was proud of how his business had grown in the relatively short time he'd lived in Maryland.

"Yes," said Molly. "We've decided to turn the unused studio space above the garage into an office. The garage is detached, so it will have a separate entrance and its own bathroom and kitchenette." Molly was a full-time author, so she worked from home and could oversee the construction that would take place.

"Sounds like a perfect set-up," said Erin.

"How's work going for you, Erin?" Asked Rick. "What's going on with that big case you've been dealing with?" He was referring to the Madison-Richards case.

"It's a nightmare. I don't think I've ever seen two more unreasonable people. The hatred they have for each other is incredible. For as much as they say they want to this to be over and done with, they are doing everything they can to drag it out longer. I just got notice the other day – the husband is now suing the wife for custody of the family cat. It was the wife's cat before they got married, and she took it when they separated, but now he's decided he wants it. Of course, I'm sure he doesn't really care – he's just doing everything he can to get under her skin."

"How long were they married?" Adam asked.

"Just under three years. Can you believe that? All

this nonsense for three years. Their marriage was so short the wife never even got around to officially changing her name," Erin shook her head. "I have to be honest though, it's all starting to wear me down. I think I need a break from family law."

"Will you leave your firm?" Asked Rick. He was worried about his daughter. She'd been under a lot of strain this past year, and he knew her job was demanding and emotionally exhausting.

"I don't know," she answered. "I'm not going to do anything right away – I need to think some things through. But I do know that I can't do this forever. I spend my entire day dealing with people who are angry, sad, you name it – it's hard to be in that type of environment day in and day out. And having just gone through my own divorce makes it harder, of course."

"Well we're here if you ever want to bounce ideas off of us or just vent." Karen reached over and gave Erin's shoulder a little shake. "We support you and whatever you decide to do. Don't forget that."

After dinner, Molly came out of the kitchen carrying the cake she'd baked. It was red velvet, one of Erin's favorite. They sang happy birthday, and as Erin blew out the candles, she wished that she'd find her path. She knew that family law, and maybe law in general, wasn't what she wanted anymore. She had so many different ideas rolling around in her head, so her birthday wish was that she'd figure out her next move, and soon.

Molly cut large slices of cake for each person as Karen scooped a healthy portion of vanilla ice cream onto each plate before it was passed around. Soon everyone was digging in – the cake was delicious. Molly was definitely the baker in the family.

"Now it's time for presents," Molly sang after everyone had finished and the dishes had been cleared.

"But first let's grab some coffee and head into the family room."

Moments later, Erin, steaming cup of coffee in her hands, made her way into the beautifully decorated family room and sank into her favorite leather chair. This room had hosted many parties, from birthdays to bridal and baby showers, to Christmas mornings with presents piled high under the tree.

"Here," said Macy as she handed Erin a gift bag stuffed with tissue paper. "This is from me, Adam, Julep, Hunter, and Fitz."

"Aww thanks. You have the sweetest children," Erin said with a wink. Inside the bag was a dark brown leather halter, complete with a brass nameplate that read "Getjazzywithit," which was Jazzy's official race name, and now, show name.

Mace! It's beautiful!"

"I figured you could use a fancy show halter, especially now that you're getting Jazzy out regularly. She needs to look like the queen she is."

"Thank you so much! It's almost too pretty to let her wear," she laughed.

Molly handed Erin her present next. It was thin and rectangular, so Erin figured it was a book of some sort. She hoped so as she, like her sister, was an avid reader.

"I hope you like it," said Molly. "I think you'll get some use out of it anyway."

Inside was a black leather-bound journal from View Halloo. At the top embossed in silver read Equestrian Competition Journal, and at the bottom was her name, Erin Sorrenson.

Erin gasped. "Molly, this is exquisite!" She quickly paged through the journal and saw that there was a place for everything – from tack and vet record keeping to show goals and competition notes. "This is absolutely gorgeous – and perfect timing too for my new partnership with Jazzy. I can't wait to fill it up!"

"Of course the writer in the family gives a journal," Macy laughed. It was a wonderful gift that Erin would cherish for a long time.

"And finally, this is from us," said Karen as she handed Erin a rather large, brightly-wrapped box. Inside was a brand new Tipperary eventer vest, hunter green in color.

"A new vest? Thank you! How did you know I needed a new one?"

"I saw your old one hanging in Macy's tack room and remembered buying that for you sometime in college. I figured it was time for an update. I'm sure the technology has improved quite a bit since then!"

"Thank you so much! I was thinking I'd get a new one sometime next year – I just haven't had the extra money recently. This is perfect – thanks mom," Erin said, getting up to hug her mother. "Thanks dad," she said, turning to embrace her father.

"It was all your mother's idea. I just hand over the credit card," Rick teased.

"Well thank you all, for everything. For being here, for the gifts. You are the best family a girl could ask for," Erin said sincerely. She had to admit that not having Kevin here with her tonight had been harder than expected, but she was grateful for such loving parents, a thoughtful and generous sister and brother-in-law, and a caring friend who was truly family as well.

Later that night, Erin and Macy walked down to the barn for their final night check on the horses. The air was crisp, but since it was early October, it wasn't too chilly, and the girls were comfortable in their jeans and lightweight jackets. Julep loped alongside them, happy for the prospect of some late-night mouse hunting in the barn.

"Thanks again for the halter – it's just gorgeous," Erin said as she slid open the main doors to the barn. The horses were already nestled in their stalls and let out a variety of sleepy nickers as the girls entered.

"You're welcome. I figure you'll get plenty of use out of it, especially in the coming year."

"I love that all the gifts were geared towards my upcoming competitions and campaigns with Jazzy. A new year calls for new goals for me and this girl," said Erin as she walked up to Jazzy and wrapped her arms around her horse's neck. In typical Jazzy fashion, who was a touch-me-not, she immediately flattened her ears and flung her head in the air. Erin, a true mare person, simply laughed.

"She's always so opinionated," laughed Macy.

"I know. But the funny thing is, she can turn around and walk away from me if she wants. But she chooses to stay here and let me love her. I think she secretly enjoys it."

"I wouldn't be surprised. Typical moody mare. She loves you but she'd rather die than admit it!"

The girls then gave each horse another flake or two of hay, topped off their water buckets, and kissed the fuzzy noses one last time before heading in.

As Erin climbed into bed a few hours later, she reflected on her day. Life was full of ups and downs, and while she had had her share of downs lately, she knew her life was too good for her to stay sad for much longer. It would be a while before she was completely over

Kevin and the life they'd shared together, but she had loving family and friends, a hobby that she loved more and more each day, and, well, she had options. While it would be a shame to leave her firm and waste her law degree, she knew in her heart that she couldn't do it much longer.

She grabbed her laptop off the nightstand and opened Google where she typed in, "Ian O'Ryan."

Immediately a bunch of results appeared on the screen with the website of his Emerald Isle Farm listed at the top. She clicked it.

Ian had been one of two professionals who had responded when she sent her working student application, and he had offered her a three month working student apprenticeship. She had turned it down in favor of law school, but now she was curious.

On a whim, and because it was her birthday – a day that marked a new year full of opportunity, Erin clicked on the Contact Me tab and located Ian's email address.

She copied it, opened her Gmail, and pasted it into a blank email. She kept it short but told him how he had accepted her working student application years ago, and how she'd be interested in applying for the same position should he have one available. She gave a brief overview of Jazzy, the work they'd done together so far, and her future eventing aspirations. Then Erin attached a few recent videos of her flatting and jumping Jazzy, and an old video of her competing with her previous mare, Ruby. She believed that that video was one she had originally sent to Ian for her initial application.

Then, before she could talk herself out of it, she hit Send.

Chapter 9

Fall in Maryland was a splendid time with its cool, crisp days, its trees putting on a breathtaking display full of reds, oranges, and yellows, and pumpkin-flavored everything everywhere you looked.

Erin kept herself busy with work and Jazzy, and she was loving the weather – it was perfect for some late afternoon schooling. Time wouldn't be changing for another three weeks, so she was still able to squeeze in some rides with Macy after work.

Jazzy was coming along brilliantly. Erin had taken her, along with Molly, Macy, and their horses, to Loch Moy Farm out west in Adamstown, Maryland, to school in their arenas. They had three large outdoor rings that all connected and were filled with both stadium and cross country jumps. They hosted cross-derbies every winter and spring, and Erin already had the December date marked on the calendar. Both Macy and Molly were coming too.

All three horses had been wonderful during their schooling sessions, and Fitz, new to jumping, popped over some cross-rails like it was nothing. Erin and Molly were schooling a little higher and were gearing toward the Beginner Novice division.

Erin, on her way home from work, stopped at her local Starbucks to grab yet another pumpkin-spiced latte. This was her third one this week, and it was Wednesday. This is becoming a bit of a problem, she thought to herself as she paid the cashier and drove off. *When did I become so basic?*

Fall was her favorite time of year, but this year she wasn't her normal self for a variety of reasons. Even though she'd unfriended Kevin on Facebook, she'd seen that he and their old group of friends, mostly his friends from college, had gone up to Pennsylvania and spent the day getting lost in one of those huge corn mazes. That was a tradition that Erin had looked forward to every year, but this year instead of her, Kevin posed for a picture with his new girlfriend.

Her heart ached a little at yet another unwanted change, but of course those were Kevin's friends he'd brought to the marriage. There was no reason they'd invite her over him. Still, she had missed out on something she truly enjoyed. They'd all always laugh at her at how seriously she'd take it. Competitive at everything she did in life, Erin always insisted that they break into two teams, boys against the girls, and whoever made it out first with all the pieces to the puzzle, won. What did they win? Well, they usually determined that on the ride up there. One year the losers had to buy the winners dinner on the way home. Another year, when they were much younger, the boys, if they lost, had to ride home without their pants on. The girls, if they lost, had to ride home without their shirts! Thankfully, the girls had won, and they had joked the whole way home about how they had, "beaten the pants off the boys!" The guys had been great sports and were more than content to drive home in only their boxers and briefs!

But life can't stay the same forever, and Erin was learning that lesson quickly.

She took a sip of her latte, relishing the flavor and waiting for the caffeine to hit, when her phone rang. It was her mom.

"Hey mom," she said as the call came through her car speakers.

"Hi, honey. What are you up to?"

"Just on my way home. Grabbed a

Starbucks…again," she giggled.

Karen laughed. "You're going to be lost when Christmas comes, and they discontinue all things pumpkin."

"I will be. Although I'll probably just move right into their gingerbread lattes."

The two chatted for a moment until Karen asked her a question that caught Erin completely off guard.

"I was wondering, and please tell me if I'm overstepping, but any chance you're ready to start dating again? The reason I ask," Karen rushed on before Erin could interrupt, "is because I ran into Susie Talbot at the tack shop today and she told me that her son, Leo, has just moved home from New York…and he's single. You remember Leo, don't you?"

"Of course I remember him. We went to school together. I haven't seen him since senior year of high school though. Mom, please tell me you didn't set me up."

"I didn't, honey, but I told her that I'd pass this info along. I think you two have quite a bit in common. He's newly-divorced himself, and he's an attorney. He was working in Manhattan but was offered a job at a firm in Hunt Valley and figured this was as good a time as any to make some changes. I think he was looking for an excuse to get out of the city and closer to home."

"Mom, I appreciate you playing match maker, but I really have no interest in dating right now."

"You don't have to think of it as a date. It could just be two old friends catching up. I know you have Macy and Molly, but you must be getting a little lonely. You said yourself that you've lost some friends throughout all this, which is only natural. It might be nice to get together with someone going through the same thing and, I don't know, just have some companionship.

Someone to do things with."

Erin had to admit that her mom was right. She was lonely, and sometimes a little bored. Kevin's friends prior to their marriage had sided with Kevin, of course. And her friends were Team Erin, as they'd said. Still, her list of people to hang out with had been cut in half.

"I'll think about it. But I can't make any promises. Besides, I'm not the best company these days anyway."

"I'm sure he feels the same way about himself. But that's fine. Think it over and let me know."

Macy was already home when Erin walked through the door and prepared to scoop up Julep as the little pup careened around the kitchen table and launched herself into Erin's arms.

"Want to go riding?" Macy asked. She had gotten off a little earlier than expected and was itching to get in the saddle.

"Absolutely. Let me change, and then I can also tell you about my mom's latest idea. She wants to set me up with this guy I went to high school with," she said as she rolled her eyes.

"Oh goodness, can't wait to hear about this one."

Jazzy and Fitz were so excited to get out and stretch their legs that the girls let them roll right into an easy canter heading towards the back of Macy's property. Then they slowed and ducked into the woods to pick up the small trail that led onto Adam's farm next door.

Erin filled Macy in on what her mom had said about Leo and asked for her advice. Should she go out with him, get her feet wet again in the world of dating…or should she get a dog instead and become a spinster? Actually, if she was heading towards spinsterhood, then she should probably get a cat instead.

"Somehow I just don't think you'll end up a

spinster," Macy laughed. "Unless you want to be, of course, because that's fine too. I know Erin Sorrenson doesn't need a man!"

"That's right! I just need my horses, and seriously maybe a dog or a cat. We should get some barn cats, by the way. I was thinking that the other day when I saw a mouse scurry through. I know we have Julep, but it would be fun to have some cats around."

"Agreed. I was thinking that the other day too. Molly recently told me about this program through the Harford Humane Society that actually specializes in placing barn cats. I think I'll give them a call. But in the meantime, what will you do about Leo?"

"I don't know. I'm intrigued. I did like him back in school – he was really popular and funny, but he was one of those genuinely nice guys. Most boys at that age are absolute assholes. But I haven't seen him in years. I think we're friends on Facebook, but that's about it."

"Maybe tell your mom that you're interested, but then leave it at that. She'll pass that along to his mom, but then the ball is in his court. If he wants to make the first move and call, great. If not, oh well."

"Good idea. I honestly can't waste any brain power on this. I know mom's worried about me though. She just wants me to find someone so I'm not alone."

"Yeah, she means well. All parents just want to see their kids happy and settled. But tell her you're not alone – you will always have me."

"And Julep?"

Macy laughed. "Yes, and Julep! She is more than happy with the split-custody arrangement we have. She loves having you around."

"Well I love being here, and I don't think I'll ever be able to thank you enough for opening up your home to me when I needed it most. You had just been through a terrible ordeal with your mother's passing. The last thing you needed was to add me to your already over-burdened shoulders." She smiled over at her friend.

"You have no idea how much you helped me. Do you know how nice it was and still is to come home to you instead of an empty house? I think we both helped each other equally."

"We are good little roommates, that's for sure."

"I love our girl talk in the evenings."

"Me too. And speaking of girl talk, I forgot to tell you something. Well, I didn't want to mention it because I don't think anything will come of it…but I emailed Ian O'Ryan a few weeks ago. I asked if he had any openings for a working student. I haven't heard back yet, and I probably won't, but I'd like to make some changes and figured focusing more on horses and my riding would be the best place to start."

"What will you do if he accepts you?"

"I think I'd take it. I'd ask for a leave of absence at my work and go for it."

"Look at you! You are spontaneously combusting, and I love it!"

"Right? It was the night of my birthday. After I went to bed, I pulled up my laptop and sent off an email before I could change my mind."

"Birthdays are good for that, aren't they? They make you re-evaluate your life and what you want that next year to look like."

"Exactly. And I want this next year to look different. I know a divorce already qualifies it as different, but you know what I mean."

"I do. And if he accepts you, I think you should take it."

Chapter 10

The following Saturday, Erin made her way over to Molly and Beau's to see the construction on Monkton Equine Medicine's new office. A few months prior to their marriage, Molly and Beau had purchased a beautiful brick colonial about five minutes away from Macy's farm, and together they had turned it into a loving home.

Located above the detached garage, the office was one large spacious room with a small bathroom tucked into the corner on the right as you entered, and a kitchenette was to the left along the side wall. The room was completely bare of furnishings, but everything was complete. It was painted a pale greyish blue with white trim. On the wall facing the back of the property, they had enlarged the two existing windows and added a sliding glass door and private deck.

"What a nice space," Erin said as soon as she walked through. "I love that you added the sliders and the deck – it's so bright and airy up here."

"Thanks," Molly said as she pointed out some of the updates. "Mr. Terry made the custom cabinets for the kitchenette as well as the vanity in the bathroom."

"He's so talented. They are just perfect." The gleaming dark cherry cabinets really popped against the light colored walls.

"I need your help with decorating," said Molly. "You know I'm hopeless."

"I'm at your service. Let's go to some consignment and antique shops and see what we can find. Actually, we could probably start in mom's attic. You know she saves everything, and I'm sure she has plenty of equestrian décor. What are you going to do about a desk?"

"Good question. I was thinking about grabbing something from IKEA, but their stuff is so modern. Maybe I'll put an 'in search of' ad on Facebook marketplace or craigslist. I want it to match the cabinets as close as possible."

"If you end up not needing an admin, you should move your office up here. Imagine this whole wall as a floor-to-ceiling bookshelf," Erin said as she pointed to the wall facing the front of the property and road.

"That's exactly what I told Beau! I said that now that this is finished and turned out beautifully, I'm calling dibs. He, however, did not find that idea as amusing as I did," she smiled.

"Have you advertised for the position?"

"Not yet. We were hoping to find someone through word of mouth. Maybe someone who's already retired but just looking to get out of the house and earn a couple extra bucks every week. That would be ideal. Or even a stay-at-home-mom who wants to work while her kids are at school during the day. Just part-time hours right now, but hopefully that changes as business grows."

"I'll start spreading the word. Hell, with a pretty office like this, maybe I'll take the job," Erin said seriously.

"I'm pretty sure your law degree can be put to better use elsewhere...like practicing law!" Molly laughed.

"I know, but I'm over it all." Erin had already told her sister about her email to Ian O'Ryan, so Molly knew that Erin was ready for something different. "I'm going to lose it if I don't make some changes soon. There were moments when I really enjoyed my job, but I can't imagine making it my entire life's work. Not anymore."

"Would you seriously want the job? It's only part-time, at least for now. I honestly think you'd be incredibly bored with it. It's night and day from the rat race you're used to at the firm."

"That's the thing – I do want something completely different. Can I think about it?"

"Absolutely. It's yours if you want it but let me know as soon as you can. Ideally, Beau would like someone in here before Christmas, after New Year's at the latest."

Erin hugged her sister. "Thank you. I appreciate it. I'll think on it and let you know in a few days. All I know for sure is that I need to get out of family law…and out of the city. I'm tired of commuting so far every day."

"If anyone understands that, it's me." Molly was a country mouse and couldn't imagine how her sister had lived and worked in the city for as long as she had. "Let me know what you decide. In the meantime, let's take a little drive over to mom's and see what's in the attic!"

The following evening Erin stood in front of the full-length mirror in her bedroom and surveyed the reflection looking back at her. Her mom had passed along her number, and surprisingly, Leo had called her the next day. They decided they'd meet for a quiet dinner that Sunday night at the Manor Tavern. Erin suggested that restaurant since it was one of her favorites – and because it was close to home. The last thing she wanted to do was drive out of her way for something she really wasn't in the mood for.

She had gone back and forth about canceling, but in the end, she decided to go forward with it. It would do her some good to get out of the house and have a nice dinner. And it would be fun to catch up with Leo. It had been ages since she'd seen him last, and there was just something about reconnecting with someone from childhood that lifted her spirits. It was always enjoyable to reminisce about the good old days.

Erin had decided on skinny jeans, black heels, and a red colored long-sleeved sweater. It was lightweight, so she added a black and white houndstooth print scarf to her ensemble. She remembered that Leo was tall, so she had chosen the three inch heels for her five foot six inch frame. While Erin had always been slender, the stress from the last year had stolen a few extra pounds from her, making her seem even more long and lithe. She added some loose curls to her light brown, medium-length hair and a little eye liner and shadow made her hazel eyes pop. She turned from left to right a few times to confirm that she looked presentable enough to be seen in public, grabbed a light jacket, and walked out the door.

As she drove the few miles to the restaurant, she realized she was neither excited nor nervous. She had zero expectations about this dinner – and that's exactly what it was – dinner, not a date. Erin was doing this more to appease her mother than anything else. But, again, she was looking forward to an evening out of the house.

The sun was setting as she pulled in and found parking in the back. Leo was already there and waiting for her outside. His face lit up when he saw her, and Erin felt the years fade away. Minus a little premature greying on his temples, he looked exactly the same – tall, dark, and handsome was a perfect description. Leo had been that funny guy in class that everyone wanted to be around, but he hadn't let his popularity go to his head. He had been nice to everyone, and Erin had always admired his confidence.

"Well you haven't changed one bit," Leo said as he walked over and pulled Erin into a tight hug.

"Neither have you!" She said genuinely. "It's so

great to see you."

Leo held the door open and Erin walked into the restaurant. As they were shown to a table in the main dining room, Leo looked around.

"I haven't been here in years. They've made a bunch of changes."

"They have, and their food still delicious."

They each ordered a glass of wine and caught up while they perused the menu. Erin had forgotten how much she had liked Leo, how easy he was to talk to, and now they had even more in common.

He had gone to Columbia for law school and then stayed in Manhattan after graduation. He had married his "law school sweetheart," as he put it, but they had called it quits early last year.

"So, I've been officially divorced for over a year now, and when Simon & Smith offered me a job, I jumped at the chance to come home. It was time. I loved living in New York, but I realized that I was exhausted. The city just got to be too much, and I missed my family."

"I feel the same way. I still work in Baltimore, but I lived in the city as well until Kevin and I separated right before the new year. Crumbling marriage excluded, I was getting claustrophobic being downtown. I needed to get back to the country, away from people and cars and high-rises. And I wanted to get another horse and start riding and competing seriously again."

They continued to chat easily throughout the entire meal, laughing about the old days and swapping stories about the people from back then whom they still kept in touch with, which wasn't too many, unfortunately.

While they waited for their coffees and dessert, Leo excused himself to use the restroom, so Erin took a moment to check her phone. She laughed when she saw a group text from Molly and Macy, both asking her how things were going and if it was love at first sight.

Things are going well – he's still really cute. I haven't been shot by any of cupid's arrows, but he's very sweet and easy to talk to.

Then she saw an email that took her breath away. It was from Ian O'Ryan.

She quickly opened it and began to read. Erin was so engrossed in it that she didn't even notice Leo's return.

"Everything okay?" He asked.

"Oh! Sorry – yes. Just work," she said quickly, not wanting to tell him what was really going on.

"Good news, I hope?"

Erin smiled broadly. "Yes, great news actually."

Here we go, she thought happily.

Chapter 11

"You got it?!" Macy squealed when Erin told her the news later that night. "What will you do? Will you go? You've GOT to go!"

Erin was beaming. "He said he wants me to move in on January 2nd and officially start on the 3rd. It's a three month contract with a potential month by month renewal after that. And I get to bring Jazzy, of course." She couldn't believe it. Not taking this position years ago was one of her biggest regrets in life, and here she was able to make it all come true. Better late than never, as they say.

"So, what's your plan? Will you quit your job or just take a leave of absence? What do you think your parents will say?" Macy was firing off questions left and right.

"Honestly I haven't thought it all through. After I sent in my application, I sort of convinced myself I wouldn't hear back, so I didn't allow myself to hope or plan. But now? It's really happening!" Erin had been given the opportunity to redo a portion of her life that she'd missed out on. She was over the moon.

"Sit down, I'll make tea. But keep talking," Macy said, busying herself in the kitchen.

"I need to think on everything a bit more, but my gut tells me to quit my job. I'm not happy with it, so why would I want to go back to it after this is over? I kind of like the idea of not knowing what's next, of not having a plan beyond the three months there. And it may even be longer, I guess, because he mentioned the month by month extension."

"Is it paid?"

"No, unfortunately, not paid. But I get free room

and board for myself and for Jazz. And I get one or two free lessons a week from Ian, and instruction should we go to an event. I have enough in the bank to tide me over until I get back. I could probably stay there close to six months and still be okay. Oh – but he did mention I would have the opportunity to make money giving lessons to some of his students, so I guess there's that."

"And your parents?"

"I think they'll be a little disappointed. I know they don't want me to waste my law degree, but I'm not wasting it per se. It will never go away – I can always become a lawyer again if I want. But overall, they just want me to be happy."

"Did you tell them that you had applied?"

"No. I figured I'd cross that bridge when I came to it…because of course I didn't really expect to hear back. But now it's here. I'm so excited, Mace. This is something I've thought about and regretted for *years*."

"Well I, for one, am so proud of you. You've been through a lot, and it takes courage to up and leave everything you've ever known…and now you've done it twice. First with Kevin and now with your job." She walked over to the table and sat a mug down in front of Erin.

"Thanks, my friend. You've been in my corner since day one, and I don't know if I could have gotten through everything without you. But now I have a favor to ask," she said with a sly smile. "Can you save my room for me?"

"You know it!" Macy sighed for a moment. "It will suck not having you here though. I'm so happy that you've been given this opportunity, but I won't lie. I'm going to miss you like crazy."

"I'm going to miss you too, but it won't be for long. Three months. I can't even think past that."

"Oh! Tell me about your date!"

"Mace, I told you it wasn't a date! It was just dinner between two old friends," Erin said. "But it was lovely, really. He's just as sweet and funny as I remembered. I can't say I felt a spark or anything magical, but we had a very nice time."

"Will you see him again?"

"Probably not, especially now that I'm going away. I'd like to keep in touch with him though. He really is a good guy. Paid for my meal too!"

"Well done!" Macy winked.

Erin called Molly later that night to fill her in on everything, and as expected, Molly was overjoyed that her sister was taking the working student position. Erin had already emailed Ian back, letting him know that she would be honored to accept and to thank him again for this opportunity.

After she and Molly hung up, Erin debated about calling her mom, but figured this was a conversation best had in person.

She pulled out her calendar – it would be November in less than a week. She decided that she'd give a month's notice to her boss immediately tomorrow morning. A month would give her enough time to transition her cases over to the other attorneys in the office and to tie up any loose ends. Then she'd have all of December to get her life in order, celebrate Christmas with her family, and then prepare to leave for The Plains, Virginia, on January 2nd.

Sitting at her desk the following morning, Erin felt an extreme sense of peace. She was about to go into one of the managing attorney's office and give her notice. She felt it down to her very core that she was heading in the right direction. The many years she'd spent with this firm had brought her highs and lows, and she'd made some friendships that she knew would last. But it was time to close this chapter and start anew.

"Honey, I can't believe it. What am I going to do without seeing your pretty little face in here every day?" Robyn asked when Erin told her the news later that morning. Her boss had taken the news well and wished her much luck. Now that he had been made aware, it was time to start telling the rest of the staff, and Robyn was the first to know.

"Thanks so much, Rob. I don't know what I'll do without you taking care of me and helping keep my life together!" She truly would miss her assistant. Not only had Robyn been amazing at her job, she had a heart of gold and looked out for Erin as if she were one of her kids. The age difference between them had allowed Robyn to take on a maternal role, and Erin knew she wouldn't have been nearly as successful here had it not been for her.

"It was my pleasure. I know you'll be successful in whatever you put your mind to, whether that's horses or eventually coming back to law. And you keep in touch, you got that?"

"You know I will. I'm so happy to be moving on, but I know I'm going to miss this place – you especially." With that, Erin came around from behind her desk and gave Robyn a tight hug.

"Now you stop that," said Robyn with a sad smile. "I'm going to be in tears if we don't stop this now. I've still got one more month with you, and I'm going to enjoy every last day. So, tell me what you need. How can I help?"

With that, they got down to business. Robyn was an assistant to two other attorneys in addition to Erin, so the cases that would be passed onto them were already on file and would be easy to transition. There were also a few cases that should be wrapped up in a month's time, so Erin would hold onto them in hopes of seeing them through to completion. There was a lot of work still to be done, and Erin knew the month would go fast. She was going to give this final month her all and go out feeling good about her work and accomplishments over the years.

Now that work was somewhat in order, Erin had one final thing to do, and that was to tell her parents.

Chapter 12

On Erin's way home from work that Monday, she swung by Molly and Beau's house to tell them the news. Beau was still out on a call, but Molly was home as she was almost every day. As a full-time writer, her home was her office, and that was just how she liked it. Erin joked that her sister could go days without leaving the house, but it was true. Molly was someone who thrived on quiet and solitude, whereas both Erin and Macy needed more social interaction.

"Hey, what a nice surprise!" Molly said as she answered the door and hugged her sister. "I was just getting dinner ready – should I add an extra place?"

"Thanks for asking, but no. I have to get home and feed the horses. I think Macy's at some event with Adam tonight."

"Well if you change your mind, I made plenty." She pointed to a crockpot containing a delicious smelling beef stew.

"I will. But I came by to tell you the news. As you know, I got the working student position, so I gave notice at the firm today. As of November 30th, I'm officially out of the family law arena, at least temporarily."

"Oh my goodness," said Molly. "You're really doing this. Erin, I'm so happy for you. You know I'll always support you one hundred percent…but are you sure?"

"Completely."

"It's just you've been through a lot lately, and I don't want you making a rash decision. Not that I think you are. I know you think things through, but I don't want you doing anything you'll regret."

"I know, and I appreciate your concern. Life has thrown a lot at me this past year, but I'm ready for this. I will absolutely lose my mind if I stay in this field much longer – and even if this ends up not being a smart move for me, I need to make a change. I'm just going to combust if I have to continue walking into that office day in and day out. I need to shed my old life, if only for a few months."

"Of course, I know what that feels like – and I ended up meeting Beau while I was doing just that in Kentucky, shedding my old life." She reached over and took her sister's hand. "You do what you have to do. I'm behind you."

"Thanks Molly. Maybe years from now I'll look back on this moment and I'll either call it the best or the stupidest thing I've ever done. Besides, I told Ian I'd be there, and I gave notice at work. What's done is done. I'm committed now, so full steam ahead!"

Molly laughed. This was the Erin she knew! "You are committed, and you're going to be amazing. You'll work with his horses and Jazzy and gain so much experience from this that you'll come back a better, stronger rider, if that's even possible. You're already the best rider I know."

"That's sweet of you to say, but I do have so much to learn. And even though I'm nervous about this move, I feel in my gut that I'm heading in the right direction. Before law school, I really contemplated making horses my life's work, but then I let society get the best of me. What was the smarter move? Furthering my education and becoming a lawyer, or becoming a horse trainer and working with thousand-plus pound animals who have minds of their own? Society told me to go to law school, and even though my heart said horses, I still went to law school. But now, I'm taking it all back.

The divorce challenged me to look at my life through fresh eyes, and damnit Moll, I'm not going to live with regrets. Not anymore."

Molly was smiling after Erin finished preaching. "I'm proud of you. It takes guts to do something like this, but you've always been the brave one in this family. I've always admired that about you. I know you're going to kill it. But the question is, will mom and dad kill you for giving up your career?" Molly laughed.

"Well they're coming over for dinner tomorrow night, so I guess we'll find out." While their parents had always encouraged their daughters to follow their hearts, they were no in way risk takers. Erin had no idea how they'd react to her news.

But at the end of the day, she was thirty-four now. She was a grown woman on a mission. She'd done it their way – college, law school, a professional career, but now she was going out on her own.

"Are you sure you want me to stay?" Asked Macy. "I can make myself scarce and stay upstairs. Or I can run over to Adam's."

"Yes, please stay. My parents will think it odd if you stay upstairs in your own home. Besides, it might soften the blow a little if you're here. You can back me up."

"I absolutely will, but if you'd rather have some family time without me, just shoot me a look and I'm out of here."

"Thanks Mace, but it will be fine. While I'd love my parents' support, I don't need it. I'm going into this next chapter of my life whether they like it or not. I'm doing this for me."

With that, the timer on the oven sounded the

alarm that the lasagna was finished. Macy put the final touches on a large salad and then set the table. Karen and Rick would be here any minute.

"Thanks for helping with dinner. You know I'm not the most skilled cook out there."

"You're welcome," said Macy. "Should I open some wine?"

"Yes, mom loves a good white wine. I think I have some already in the fridge. Let's get them drunk before I tell them!" Erin laughed.

The doorbell rang, and Julep howled and sprinted to the front door.

"Here we go!" Sang Erin as she went to let her parents in.

After hugging the girls and fussing over Julep, Karen and Rick sat down at the table. Erin had just pulled the garlic bread out of the oven and placed it in the center of the table.

"This looks delicious honey." Rick smiled at his daughter. "Thanks for having us over."

They all chatted a bit while everyone passed around plates to be loaded with the Italian goodness. The lasagna tasted just as wonderful as it looked, so they all dove right in.

Karen, who had the feeling that something was up, smiled slyly at her daughter. "So, what's the special occasion?"

"Can't a daughter make dinner for her parents without it being a special occasion?"

Rick laughed. "Yes, Molly can. But not you – not our daughter who hates to cook."

Erin laughed at that one. "Okay, you got me. Here goes." She took a deep breath and sat down her silverware. "Dad, you might not remember this, but mom, you will. Remember after college I had applied to be a working student for a few professional riders?"

"Oh yes," Karen answered. "And if I'm not mistaken, two of them accepted you."

"Yes, one of them was Ian O'Ryan in The Plains, Virginia. He owns Emerald Isle Farm. Anyway, turning down that offer to go to law school instead has been one of the biggest regrets of my life. So, on a whim a few weeks ago, I emailed Ian and asked if he had any working student positions available now, and not only did he have one open, but he accepted my application. Jazzy and I leave for Virginia on January 2nd."

Her parents were both silent for a few moments.

"What about your job at the firm?" Rick finally asked.

"I quit. Yesterday, as a matter of fact, I handed in my letter of resignation. I gave one month's notice, and then I'll take December to get some things in order and enjoy the holidays. After that, I head to Virginia for three months as per my contract with Ian."

"So, this is already a done deal? Everything's been decided?" Asked Karen. Both of her parents wore very worried expressions as Erin knew they would.

"Yes, it is, and I couldn't be happier about it. I know this probably isn't what you want for me, but I need this. I need to take off for a bit and do something that I love. It won't be forever – just three months."

"And then what?" Asked her father.

"Then I don't know. For the first time in my life, my future is uncertain – and honestly, I feel pretty great. Maybe I'll start my own law firm. Maybe I'll do something completely different, but whatever it is, I'll figure it out then."

"I wish you would have come to us first," said Karen, her eyes full of concern.

"Why? So you could have talked me out of it?"

"Erin, you have years and years of education that you're throwing aside," said her father. "We just don't want you making any decisions you'll regret."

"Dad, I know. But I haven't been happy at work for years. Regardless of the divorce and regardless of wanting to do the horse thing for a while, I needed a change and the timing's right. Besides, my education isn't going anywhere. I can always get a job at another firm."

"What do you think about this?" Karen asked Macy who had been sitting silently watching the exchange. Macy knew her parents, had they still been alive, would have responded exactly the same way. And she was basically in Erin's boat – she had a career that had required eight full years of schooling.

"I think it's a great idea. And I'm not just saying that because Erin is one of my best friends. She's gone through a lot this past year and needs a change of scenery. And this checks something off of her bucket list too. Not taking this position years ago was something that's always bothered her. Now she can say she did it, and during this time, she can also think about her next move. She'll always have a home here with me too, no matter what she decides." She looked over at her friend and winked.

"We just worry, that's all," said Karen. As a horse person, she could absolutely see the allure of working with someone like Ian O'Ryan, especially now that Erin had a young horse she wanted to bring along and start campaigning. But she was also worried about her daughter's future. Her job at the firm had been well-paying and stable.

"Mom, I know you do. And I'm sorry I kept you guys in the dark about this, but it's something I want to do. It's something I *have* to do. And I'll figure out my next steps after and will land on my feet. I always do," she said with confidence.

"We know you will. And whatever you need, let us know," said her father. "But please don't keep anymore life-changing secrets from us again," he said with a smile. He trusted his daughter to do what was best for her. Even though this wasn't exactly the path he'd like her to go down, she was an adult, after all, and this was her life to live.

Chapter 13

The month of November flew by. Erin ended up working late almost every day in preparation for her departure. She had cases to close and finalize and others to transition. In between the chaos, she packed up her desk, little by little, and set her sights on the horizon ahead. Maybe, if she played her cards right, she'd never work in an office like this again. She had a tiny idea rolling around in her head, but she'd need to see where life took her before she could make it a reality.

Before Erin knew it, Thanksgiving had come and gone, and she was getting ready to enter her last week of work at the firm. *I only have to do this drive three more times*, she thought happily on her way in.

By this point, her office was bare of everything except her phone, a few last files, and her computer. Seeing her space so empty made her feel a little sad, but as soon as she thought about her future and how she'd be working with horses every day, she perked right up.

She was making detailed notes on one of only a few more cases left to be transitioned when her cell beeped with a notification. It was a text from Leo. They'd swapped a few messages here and there, but she hadn't seen him since their one and only dinner in October.

L: Hey! How are you? I ran into your mom last night at the store and she told me you're moving to Virginia. Are you free for dinner tonight? Would love to catch up.
E: Yes, I meant to tell you. Things have been so busy. Tonight works. Where would you like to meet?
L: Barrett's Grill in Hunt Valley work for you?
E: Love it there. 6:30?

L: Perfect. Looking forward to it.
E: Great, see you then.

Erin realized she was smiling to herself as she added the dinner appointment into her calendar. While she was in no place to start a relationship, she had enjoyed Leo's company. He was someone with whom she could be herself, and it helped that he was getting out of a marriage too. Neither were in any rush to make commitments they weren't ready to keep.

A lunch meeting, a bunch of calls, and before Erin knew it, it was 4:00 o'clock in the afternoon. She decided she'd call it a day early so she had time to run home and change before meeting Leo.

Macy was still at work when Erin pulled into the drive about forty-five minutes later, so she fed Julep and the horses. As usual, the horses ate with gusto, digging into their grain as if they hadn't eaten in days. Erin let herself into Jazzy's stall and stroked the horse's neck while she munched on her feed. As usual, at Erin's approach Jazzy pinned her ears. *This horse*, Erin laughed to herself. All bark and no bite.

Erin pulled a hoof pick from the brush caddy out in the aisle and picked Jazzy hooves while the horse was still distracted by her meal.

"You and I have about another month here, and then we take off on an adventure," she told the mare as she worked her way around to each hoof. "It's going to be a big change, for both of us, but I think we'll do okay. And if we don't? Well, it's only three months. We'll come home and start fresh in another direction."

Erin finished with Jazzy's hooves and gave the horse a last pat before heading to throw dinner hay. Macy would check on them again when she got home, but for now they were settled in their stalls and content with their food.

Back up in her room, Erin changed out of her barn clothes and into some nice jeans and a sweater. She laughed when she realized she was wearing basically the same thing as when she and Leo met before. She pulled off the sweater and instead chose a silky sleeveless top which she paired with an informal suit jacket. The heels she had worn to work earlier were still out, so she slipped them back on. A light refresh of eye liner, mascara, and lipstick and she was good to go.

Before she walked out the door, she texted Macy to let her know her plans and that all the animals had been fed.

"It's so great to see you," said Leo as he walked over and gave Erin a kiss on the cheek. "You look lovely, as always."

"Thanks, it's good to see you too," she said. He was still wearing the suit he had obviously worn to work that day, and she had to admit that he looked very handsome. He had taken off his tie though and had unbuttoned the top two buttons of his shirt, which gave him a casual look that suited his boyish charm.

"Thanks for suggesting this place," Erin said as they were led to their table. "I haven't been here in a while, but it's one of my favorites."

"It's no problem at all. My office is across the street, so we come here often for lunch. I know you live kind of close, so I figured this was a central location."

After they looked through the menu and placed their orders, Leo got down to business.

"Okay, so tell me about this move to Virginia.

Your mom mentioned that it's only for three months, so I won't pretend I'm not happy about that. I was glad to hear you weren't leaving for good."

"Definitely not leaving for good. I'm on a three month contract that can then be re-upped on a month-by-month basis after that, both parties willing, of course. But I can't think that far ahead." Erin continued on to tell him about the position, how she had turned it down initially all those years ago, and how the timing was right to take a break from law.

"Actually, I got the news that I'd been accepted when we were at dinner last time. You had gone to the restroom when I checked my phone and saw the email."

"I remember you saying you had just gotten some good news. Well, I'm sad that I won't be able to see you for a while, but this sounds like a great opportunity. And even better that you're getting your chance now after you turned it down before. Sounds like it was meant to be."

"That's kind of how I feel too. After the three months are up, I truly have no idea what I'm going to do next, but I kind of feel at peace about it. Normally I'd be stressed beyond belief, but after the year I've had, I'm cutting myself some slack. And it also feels good to get back to my first love – horses."

"You always were that horse crazy girl in school," Leo smiled.

"Thankfully we live in a horsey area or I wouldn't have had any friends!"

"I'm pretty sure a sweetheart like you would always have plenty of friends," Leo smiled.

The rest of the dinner was lovely. The food was delicious, just as Erin remembered it to be, and the conversation was even better. By the end of the night, Erin was almost sad that she was leaving right when this, whatever *this* was, with Leo was starting. But she wasn't going to put too much thought into it. This was her time now, and she wasn't going to let anything distract her.

As they walked across the parking lot, he reached down and took her hand, and Erin was surprised by how comfortable it felt. When they reached her car, he leaned down and gently kissed her, and Erin kissed him back with more passion than she had intended.

His eyes were sad when they pulled away. "I still have another month with you, right? You said you're not leaving until January?"

"Yes, that's right. One more month." And they kissed again.

Chapter 14

It was a chilly yet sunny day in early December. Erin and Macy were up at four o'clock in the morning to prepare for the day's cross derby competition at Loch Moy Farm.

The previous week had been Erin's last at the law firm, so she was seeing life through new eyes as she pulled Jazzy out of her stall and began grooming. She had to admit that she would miss some of her colleagues, but when she handed over her badge used to gain access into the building to her boss on that last day, all she felt was relief. She was making the right decision, and she couldn't wait for this fresh start.

Erin felt her phone buzz and saw a text from Molly.

"Uh oh, Molly's not going today. She said Gypsy's thrown a shoe, so she'll have to scratch."

"Oh no," said Macy. "How typical. Horses ruin everything." She couldn't count how many times she'd had that happen to her.

"Gypsy probably saw Molly getting the trailer ready and pried her shoe off last night," Erin joked. "She said she's still coming with us, mom too, and will be over with the trailer in a few."

Erin would be competing in the Beginner Novice division which contained seventeen jumps across all three rings. None of the jumps would be higher than 2'7". Macy would be in the Elementary division with fifteen 2' jumps across the same three rings. Cross derbies were an excellent way to start preparing a horse for the types of jumps they'd see out on a cross country course. Both girls would be jumping a combination of stadium jumping verticals and oxers as well as cross country logs, coops, and maybe even a small ditch for Erin.

The girls had taken the horses to Loch Moy to school a few months prior, so both would be familiar with the rings and fences they'd be going over today. Neither had ever competed in a cross derby before though, and Erin especially was so excited. This was her last competition before heading south to Ian's, so she was determined to put in a good showing.

After both horses were groomed to perfection, the girls put light sheets on them and put them back in their stalls until Molly and Karen arrived with the trailer.

"It's crowded," Karen stated as she pulled into Loch Moy almost two hours later. There were quite a few trailers in the parking area, and the rings were already busy with competitors warming up their mounts.

"The weather has held out pretty well," said Erin from the front passenger seat. "People are probably anxious to get one final show in before winter." In just two weeks, winter would officially arrive and leave the Mid-Atlantic area blanketed with snow, freezing rain, and just overall cruddy weather until mid-March, at best.

"Well let's get these kids off the trailer and ready to go," said Macy as soon as Karen had found a nice place to park.

Everyone quickly went to work unloading the horses, walking them for a few minutes to stretch their legs, and then pulling out grooming supplies and tack. Molly went to the registration office to notify the show secretary that Erin and Macy had arrived and to grab their numbers.

"Okay, here you guys go," said Molly as she handed the girls their numbers. "Macy, you go on at

10:25, so you have almost an hour. Erin, you're on at noon."

Jazzy was much calmer than she'd been at the Olney show earlier in the fall, and Fitz was his usual relaxed self. Both girls were encouraged by their horses' laidback demeanors and eager to get in the ring.

"I still can't believe I'm heading into the wild world of eventing," said Macy. With Hunter, she had focused solely on dressage.

"You'll love it," Erin grinned. "I promise once you're hooked, you'll never look back."

"I have to agree with that," said Molly. She, too, was relatively new to eventing but already loved it.

"You two are hunter princesses and dressage queens turned eventers. Welcome to the dark side!" Laughed Erin.

Erin and Macy gave their horses each another light grooming and then tacked up. There was a large field nearby where they decided to warm up Jazzy and Fitz, and each horse trotted and cantered for a bit to limber up their long legs. A few minutes later, it was almost time for Macy to enter the ring for her round.

"I'm nervous," she admitted as the group walked towards Ring One where she'd enter and begin her course. "I know he'll be okay, but this is the first time we've jumped in a competition."

"First time for everything," Erin sang. She gave her friend a wink and then added, "You'll be fine. Fitz lives to please you, so you guys will do great. If I were you, I wouldn't even worry about the optimum time – just get around cleanly. We're both still just here to have good experiences."

"True, but I've got my stopwatch on, so if I think about it, I'll glance down every so often. Even if I don't change my pace, I want to get into the habit of checking my time as I'm riding."

"Macy Holland and F. Scott Fitzgerald, you are on deck," said the ring steward. Another competitor had just entered the ring, so Macy was next.

A few minutes later it was Macy's turn and she trotted briskly into the ring as the others echoed their wishes of good luck.

Macy heeled Fitz into a canter just prior to the first jump, and off they went. Fitz was listening to Macy's every command as they cleared a small cross-rail and then a vertical. The pair chugged happily along as Fitz flew over a coop, a rolltop, and a log – all with room to spare. One look at the grin on Macy's face and it was clear she and her horse were having a blast. Fitz's ears, pricked forward looking towards his next obstacle, along with his gleaming grey coat, appeared the picture of health and contentment. He had come a long way from the injured, newly-retired racehorse Macy had rescued.

When Macy cleared the final jump, she and Fitz were met with cheers and applause from her fan club: Erin, Molly, and Karen. She looked down at her stopwatch as she exited the ring.

"About ten seconds over the optimum time – I'll take it!"

"You two looked amazing!" Gushed Molly. "Fitz is a natural born jumper. He cleared everything easily with room to spare."

Macy dismounted and gave her horse a big hug. "We did it, big guy! I'm so proud of you!"

They then headed back to the trailer to cool out Fitz. Erin would re-tack Jazzy in about an hour, and then it would be time for them to take a spin around the ring.

When Fitz was untacked, Macy threw his sheet back on and walked along with Erin and Jazzy. Erin was trying to keep Jazzy limber before her round and keeping her moving also helped to keep the mare's mind focused on Erin and the task at hand. Like a typical Thoroughbred, Jazzy didn't like standing still and being idle, especially at a show where there was a lot of commotion.

Not too long after, it was time for Erin to mount up and head to the ring. Unlike Macy, Erin was trying to stay within the optimum time. She still wanted Jazzy to have a good experience, but Erin planned to check her watch multiple times and, as long as Jazzy was willing, slow her down or speed her up accordingly. It would be a good test of Jazzy's ability to listen and rate as Erin made adjustments. However, if they got in the ring and Jazzy went a bit rogue, then Erin would throw her strategy aside and instead focus on just having a clean, safe round.

As soon as Erin asked for the canter, she knew her horse was with her. Jazzy's pace was strong, but not quick, and she was listening to her rider. *What a good brain you have*, Erin thought as they cleared their second jump.

After their fifth jump, they headed into the second ring where they'd jump seven more before heading down a slight bank and into the third and final ring where five more jumps awaited.

Erin was in heaven as Jazzy correctly swapped her lead and headed for a small ditch. She flew over without a second glance, and Erin knew she had a brave horse on her hands. Jazzy was born for eventing.

A quick glance at her watch showed Erin that they were making great time, no need to slow down or speed up. Jazzy's pace was just right.

They made their way around the third ring and Erin finally allowed herself to smile as they headed for the final jump, a log coop. One well-timed leap and they were up and over.

"Two seconds under!" Karen shouted as Erin trotted out of the ring. "Well done!" Even though her daughters were all grown up, Karen loved the role of horse show mom and was her girls' biggest cheerleader.

"Jazzy, you were amazing!" Erin said as she patted her horse on the neck. "We make a pretty great team, don't we girl?"

On the ride home later that day, Erin's blue first place ribbon and Macy's white fourth place ribbon hung from the air freshener attached to the rearview mirror. It had been a wonderful day, and Erin couldn't wait to get to Virginia and start some serious training with her mare.

Chapter 15

"All packed?" Macy asked as she leaned against the doorframe of Erin's room.

"Yep, just about," she answered as she zipped a suitcase. It was New Year's Day and Erin was going over her checklist to make sure she hadn't forgotten anything.

Before Erin knew it, the month of December, Christmas, all the holiday festivities had come and gone, and it was time to pack for her adventure down south. The Plains was about two and a half hours from her home in Monkton, but it was a horsey area and Erin was sure she'd feel at home there in no time.

Her parents had thrown her a going away party the night before, and Molly, Beau, Macy, and Adam were also there to say goodbye and ring in the New Year. Her mom had shed a few tears as she brought out a cake for Erin to cut, but Erin couldn't help but laugh.

"Please don't cry, mom! I'm only going away for three months; I'll be back before you know it. Besides, you can drive down and visit me at any time." She gave her mom a tight hug and then turned to embrace her dad.

Now it finally feels real, she thought as she plopped one last bag on the bed, the final one to be packed. Erin had packed her mom's trailer the day before, so Jazzy was all ready to go as well. Tomorrow morning she'd load up the horse, and they'd hit the road.

"What time is Leo coming over?" Macy asked.

"He said he'd be over around six, and he's bringing pizza." Leo had called the night before to wish her a happy new year and suggest they get together one last time before Erin's departure. She'd been so busy over the last month preparing that she hadn't had much of a chance to connect with him.

"Well I'll make sure I'm out of the way by then. Adam's picking me up for a date night."

"Fun! What are you guys doing?"

"Just dinner, and then maybe a little cuddle time back at his place," she said with a wink.

"Well don't think you have to stay away on my account. This is your house – and it's not like Leo and I are an item or anything. He just wanted to catch up a bit before I leave."

"Catching up? Is that what they're calling it now?" Macy teased.

Erin threw a shirt she was about to pack at Macy. "You're bad! I like him, and if I weren't going away, I might want to explore something a little more than friendship, but it wouldn't make sense to start anything now."

"Are you going to sleep with him?"

"What is this – twenty questions?"

Macy grinned. "Just giving you a taste of your own medicine."

"You're right. I would ask you these questions if the tables were turned." She thought for a moment. "Would I like to sleep with him? Yes. Will I? Probably not."

"Well I'll probably spend the night at Adam's, so you won't have to worry about me coming home and interrupting anything."

"Thank you, my friend. Now go away," Erin laughed. "You're distracting me with all this sex talk! Other than that night with Kevin around my birthday, it's been a lonely year."

"In the words of the great, all-knowing Erin, 'You do you,'" said Macy.

"That is some sage advice. I'm full of it, aren't I?"

Erin replied, shaking her head and giggling. She was certainly good at giving advice, but would she take it?

Two hours later there was a knock at the door. Julep barked to alert Erin, but of course she was expecting company.

"Hi, thanks for coming," said Erin as she opened the door to find Leo holding a pizza box and a couple of take-out bags.

"Of course, thanks for having me. I know this was short notice," he said as he leaned over and gave Erin a kiss on the cheek.

She led Leo to the kitchen which was in the back of the house. Julep careened around, happy to have a visitor who was full of new smells. She sniffed Leo's legs, and when he bent down to give her a little pet, she licked his nose.

"You're a friendly girl, aren't you?"

"She's Macy's. It's going to take everything I have not to steal her when I leave tomorrow. I think I'm going to miss her most of all."

"I don't blame you – she's very sweet," he said as Julep rolled over on her back, offering her stomach for some belly rubs. Leo happily obliged.

"When I come back, I think I'll get my own dog so I don't have to share with Mace. On some of my lonelier nights, I'll knock on Macy's bedroom door, scoop Julep up, and snuggle with her in bed."

"I hope you're having less and less of those nights, especially as you get further away from the divorce."

"I am, thankfully. And this new change of scenery will help too."

They sat down at the table in the kitchen and each

pulled out a slice of pizza. "I got some fries, onion rings, and bread sticks," said Leo. "I didn't know what you liked, so I got a little of everything."

"Well I like everything, so thank you. Fries especially," she said as she added a handful of fries to her plate. She looked up at Leo and gave him a smirk. "We're friends, right?"

"Of course we are."

"And friends don't judge each other, right?"

"Right. Where are you going with this?"

"Well, I'm about to do something most people find unbelievably gross," said Erin as she got up and went over to the refrigerator. "I love to dip my fries in mayonnaise," she said, looking back over her shoulder to see Leo's reaction.

He started to laugh. "I will say I think that's a first for me but bring it over here and let me try it. First time for everything."

Erin laughed as she sat the mayo on the table between them. "Good! I was afraid I'd scare you off."

"Takes a lot to scare me away," he said as he dipped a fry in the mayonnaise. "Not too bad, honestly. I can see the appeal." He dipped another fry, then another.

"I think I've converted you! Cheers!" She said as they toasted with fries loaded with mayo.

Dinner with Leo was the perfect way to start the New Year, Erin thought. She hadn't remembered him being so funny, but he had her laughing all through the meal. When they were finished, Erin made them hot chocolate with homemade whipped cream.

"I can't take credit for the whipped cream," she said as she spooned it out. "Molly was over the other day and made it. She's the cook in our family."

"It's delicious. My compliments to the chef."

As the night grew shorter, Erin found herself

incredibly sad that she'd soon be saying goodbye to Leo for three months. While she knew she'd be working hard and keeping busy, three months was a fairly long time.

He must have been thinking along the same lines because he said, "I'll miss you. I know you won't miss me as much as Julep, but I hope we can keep in touch. Would it be okay if I called you occasionally?"

"Absolutely. I hope you will. I'm sure I'll have some free time and won't know what to do with myself."

"Good. I look forward to those calls then."

When Leo got up to leave, they shared another passionate kiss. He gently took Erin's face in his hands and pulled her close. He kissed her softly and tantalizingly slow, and Erin was tempted to move everything up to her bedroom. But she decided against it and eventually, regretfully, pulled away. There will be plenty of time for that later, she thought. Or at least she hoped there would be.

"Hope that kiss will be enough to last until you get back," Leo whispered in her ear.

Chapter 16

Karen and Molly pulled in the driveway, horse trailer in low, at precisely eight o'clock that next morning. Erin was in the barn readying Jazzy for the journey when Macy walked in.

"Good morning!" She sang as she entered the barn and grabbed a wheelbarrow. Erin had already fed the horses and mucked Jazzy's stall. Macy would turn her boys out as soon as Jazzy left.

"Good morning," Erin said with a smile. She was glad that Macy was home from Adam's in time to see her off and say goodbye. "Hey mom, Molly," she called as her mom and sister also entered the barn.

"Hi dear," Karen said as she walked over and gave her daughter a hug. "Ready to go on an adventure?"

With a final hug to Macy, Hunter, Fitz, and Julep, of course, Erin loaded Jazzy onto the trailer and the three Sorrenson ladies hit the road. Karen and Molly were in the truck pulling the horse trailer, and Erin was driving separately so she'd have her own car while she was away.

They made great time and just over two and a half hours later, they were nearing their destination. With the Blue Ridge Mountains within view, and the quaint equestrian town of Middleburg just behind them, the girls knew they were in quintessential Virginia horse country.

"Oh look, there's Tri County Feeds. I haven't been there in years," said Karen as they came to a stop at an intersection in the town of Marshall. "Molly, maybe you and I will swing by there on our way home."

They made a left onto Route 55 and immediately

saw signs for The Plains. The GPS told them there were only five minutes away from Ian's farm. As they passed through the tiny town, Erin took in the small café and coffee shop on the main street and figured she'd become a regular fixture there for the next few months. The area around them was so open, much more so than back home, and Erin truly felt as if she was in the country.

"Okay, here we are," said Karen as she slowed the truck and trailer and made a left into Ian's driveway. There was a small white-colored sign with Emerald Isle Farm written in hunter green lettering. A silhouette of a horse was jumping a shamrock. They had arrived at Erin's new home for the next three months.

"Here goes nothing," Erin whispered to herself as she pulled in just behind her mom and sister. She picked up her phone and quickly called Molly. "Ian's email said to pull past the house and park in front of the smaller of the two barns."

The house, a large white colonial, was on the right side of the driveway. The drive continued straight, but part of it veered off to form a circle in front of the house where an SUV and a sedan were parked.

Behind the house was a small fenced in yard, most likely for dogs, and then a white barn, trimmed in green, stood prominently in the center of the backyard. It was your typical center-aisle barn complete with hay loft, and Erin knew from her emails with Ian that it had twelve stalls, one of which would belong to Jazzy.

As soon as they parked, a young woman walked out of the barn and headed towards Erin. The girl was short and thin with dark brown, wavy chin-length hair. She was dressed in a winter coat, schooling breeches, half chaps, and paddock boots.

"You must be Erin, welcome to Emerald Isle. I'm Laney Fox." She and Erin shook hands.

"Nice to meet you. This is my mom, Karen, and sister, Molly," Erin said, pointing to her mom and sister who had just gotten out of the truck. Laney quickly shook hands with each of them.

"Well let's get your horse unloaded and settled into her stall." Laney was friendly enough but was all business. Erin appreciated this direct manner as she, too, was very matter of fact. Her initial assessment was that the two would get along well. They might not be best friends, but they'd have a good working relationship – at least she hoped so.

Jazzy backed off the trailer easily and then stood for a moment taking in the new sights, sounds, and smells. She let out a loud whinny to which multiple horses responded. Before she started jigging in place, Erin asked her to walk on. Whenever a horse started to get antsy, it was always best to give them a task and refocus that energy as quickly as possible.

"Right this way," Laney called over her shoulder as she led them up the walkway into the barn. "Jazzy's stall is the last one on the right. It's already made up with bedding, hay, and water."

"Thank you so much," said Erin as she led her mare behind Laney. As usual, Jazzy walked confidently alongside Erin, but her ears were moving back and forth trying to pick up the sounds of the other horses nearby.

"Everyone's turned out at the moment, but I left Jester in his stall over here so Jazzy wouldn't be alone," she said as she pointed to a bay gelding in the stall directly across from Jazzy's. "He's my personal horse. Once Jazzy settles, we can turn them out."

"Sounds good to me. Thanks for leaving a friend in for her."

"The tack and feed room is at the front of the barn. I've left some empty spots for your saddle and gear.

After you've moved everything in, come find me and I'll show you to your quarters. I'll be in the main barn finishing a few chores." With a quick smile, Laney turned and walked out, heading for an enormous barn and attached indoor ring which was a short walk down a path but directly behind this smaller barn.

Behind and to the left of the large barn was a big outdoor sand ring. Paddocks and fenced fields of various sizes surrounded these structures, and way in the distance, Erin could make out cross country jumps. This was a first-class facility that had everything an eventer would need.

Karen and Molly helped Erin bring in Jazzy's grain and supplements, as well as Erin's tack and trunk. Once everything was settled, Erin turned to hug her family goodbye.

"I'd better go find Laney and see where my room is. Thank you both so much for trailering me down here and helping get things settled."

"We'll miss you so much," said Karen, eyes glistening from unshed tears.

"You're going to love it here," said Molly. "I'm actually quite jealous; I should have volunteered to come along with you, but somehow I don't think Beau would have been on board with that," she laughed.

Erin waved her mom and sister off and headed inside to check on Jazzy. Her mare appeared relaxed and was munching contentedly at her hay net in the corner.

"Well someone looks comfortable," Erin said to her horse. Jazzy had already rolled in her bedding and had clearly made herself at home, which pleased Erin.

The main barn was perfect. Erin walked inside and gave her eyes a moment to adjust to the darker space. There was a center aisle here as well, but the barn was easily triple in size. Halfway down the aisle on the left side there was a large opening that led into the attached indoor arena. On the other side of the indoor was a section for hay storage.

"Hello?" Erin called out.

"In here," came Laney's voice about halfway down on the right. "In the tack and feed room."

The room was more of a lounge. It was large enough to accommodate rows and rows of saddles and bridles along the far wall, and feed bins lined the front. Ribbons, trophies, and other various awards hung proudly on the walls. A few couches and a table and chairs filled the center of the room, and a small kitchenette was on the right. And, most importantly, the room was heated, which felt amazing on this cold January day.

"What a nice space," said Erin as she admired the room and its furnishings.

"We love it. Warm in the winter and cool in the summer. Don't know what we'd do without it." Laney was cleaning a saddle and she continued to work as she spoke. "How's Jazzy?"

"Already acting like she owns the place," Erin smiled.

"Good, that's what we like to hear. Just let me finish up and I'll show you to your quarters upstairs. You and I have apartments above the stalls. Cooper, the assistant trainer who also happens to be Ian's cousin, has that little house outside. Not sure if you noticed it on your way in. It's kind of tucked behind some trees to the right of the main house."

"No, I hadn't seen it. Is there anyone else besides us and Cooper?"

"Not at the moment. We're a little light on horses – only twenty in training, not including our personal mounts. We also have five retirees who either get lightly worked or not at all. So including ours and Cooper's mare, Lucy, there are twenty-eight horses on the farm. Not every horse is ridden every day, but Cooper and I ride most. Ian rides too, of course, but he doesn't get on as many as we do."

"Can you give me a rundown of my daily responsibilities?"

"Sure. Of course, Ian is in charge and may change things, and Cooper is second in command. I, like you, am a working student, but I've been here just over a year now. We start feeding around six-thirty every morning, then the horses go out to their fields. The ones on the schedule to be worked come in, are exercised, and then go back out until we feed dinner around five in the evening. Paul comes in Monday through Friday and mucks stalls and has a variety of other maintenance-type duties. We are responsible for our own horse's stall every day, and we're responsible for all of them on the weekends. We get around a day and a half off every week, and that day varies depending on schedules. It's kind of a play it by ear sort of thing."

"That sounds good to me. What else should I know?"

"Cooper, for the most part, will assign which horses you'll ride every day. Check that board each morning," she said pointing to a dry erase board hanging above the feed bins. "You can ride your horse at the end of the day when the others have been ridden and cared for. As part of your working student benefits, Ian will give you one lesson a week, sometimes two if you have an event coming up and need additional work."

"I'm really looking forward to that. I haven't had a lesson in years."

Laney laughed. "You might regret saying that – Ian can be a drill sergeant at times. But he's the best."

"What's he like to work for?"

"He's tough, but he's fair. I was a working student for a few other people before coming here, and he's the best by far. He'll work you to death but he's not a dick. He truly wants us to improve and leave here better than when we came. But I suppose that's typical of someone at his level. He's done it all – the Olympics, Pan Ams, you name it. He's kind of at the point where he just wants to give back to the sport he loves so much. It's not as much about the competitions anymore – he's more interested in training others now."

"He sounds like a great guy. What about Cooper?"

"Cooper's nice too, just really quiet. Coop's younger than Ian though, so he still has more to prove, if you know what I mean. He's driven and that can sometimes come across as a little arrogant, but he's not."

"I'm really looking forward to working with everyone."

"We're happy to have you," Laney said as she gave the saddle a final polish. "Okay let's show you to your room. Where are your bags?"

"Out in the aisle. I only have a few."

Laney grabbed a large suitcase while Erin picked up a smaller one and her duffel bag. Just beyond the tack room was a set of stairs that led to four apartments. They were each laid out exactly the same.

"This one's mine," Laney said as she pointed to the first door on her right. "And this one's yours," said she as they came to the second. "The others are empty at the moment."

Inside was a small kitchenette on the left with a table and two chairs. Opposite was a bathroom with a sink, mirror, toilet, and shower – no tub. In the back was a couch, little coffee table, twin bed, and dresser. A tiny closet was to the left of the bed.

"This is perfect," said Erin. Truly, it was all she needed. On the back wall were two large windows that looked out over the rest of the property. They let in plenty of light, and Erin was sure she'd be happy here.

"Great. I'll let you get settled then. When you're done, come out and I'll show you which field will be Jazzy's. She'll go out with Cooper's mare."

Chapter 17

It didn't take long for Erin to unpack her belongings. Not only was she a light traveler, but she wasn't going to be doing much other than riding, so her bags were full of breeches, socks, sweatshirts, and vests. Other than a few pairs of jeans and some nicer shirts she wouldn't wear while riding, the only other apparel she'd brought was her show clothes. She was hoping to make it to a few events during these three months.

Jazzy had settled in well. After Erin had unpacked, she'd gone downstairs to meet Laney and turn her mare out. She was in a field with Cooper's mare, Lucy, and the two squealed for a moment, and then they were fast friends. Lucy was very docile, so Jazzy instantly asserted her dominance, and that was that.

Later that afternoon Erin had volunteered to help with evening feeding, but Laney had insisted that Erin wasn't starting until tomorrow and had told her to go relax.

"We have every intention of working you to the bone, so go take advantage of the down time," Laney had laughed.

When Erin walked back into her room, she realized that she hadn't brought any personal touches, which was unfortunate. No framed photos, no books, nothing. Maybe she'd ask her mom to send her some things from home.

She also realized that she didn't have any food, so she made her way downstairs again to ask Laney where the closest grocery store was. Erin would grab some staples like milk and cereal, and then figure out a few simple things to make for dinner. Breakfast for dinner was always an easy option and sandwiches for lunch would work out well. It was times like this that she wished she was a bit more skilled in the kitchen.

"Laney?" Erin called as she made her way down the aisle.

"She's in the far field bringing in horses," answered a male voice tinged with a thick Irish accent. "You must be Erin. I'm Cooper – nice to meet you."

A tall, thin red-headed man walked over to her and extended his hand. He was well over six foot, long and lean, and Erin, at 5'6", felt tiny by his side. Cooper was attractive in that rugged, outdoorsy way. Like most red-heads, he had a smattering of freckles across the bridge of his nose, but his face held the color of someone who worked outside most days.

"Yes, hi, it's great to meet you as well. I'm really looking forward to working together."

"I saw your mare in the field – nice looking animal."

"Thank you. I have high hopes for her."

"Laney will be back in a few moments, but is there something I can do for you?"

"Yes, actually, I was just wondering where the closest grocery store was. I brought absolutely no food along."

Cooper told her where she could find the store and then went back to evening chores. "See you tomorrow," he called over his shoulder.

Nice enough guy, Erin thought as she made her way to her car. Not super chatty, but friendly enough. This will work out just fine, she thought with a smile.

When Erin returned home later that night, she stopped in to check on Jazzy one last time. Cooper must have brought her in at the same time as his mare. Jazzy was munching on hay and blissfully ignoring her mother at the door. Erin laughed to herself as she then made her way to her room, arms loaded down with grocery bags.

Once inside, she put the food away and pulled out a frying pan to make an omelet. The kitchenette already contained the basics like plates, bowls, silverware, and a variety of pots and pans for cooking. As she was mixing the eggs together and setting out the tomatoes, mushrooms, and cheese that she'd fold into the omelet, her phone began to ring – it was Macy.

"Hey Mace! I'm making dinner so I'm going to put you on speaker, okay?"

"Sounds good to me. How's everything going? All settled in?"

"Yes, just about. I'm all unpacked, and I just got back from the store where I picked up some groceries. I have a little kitchenette in my room with a cooktop. No oven, but it's not like I really know how to use one anyway," she laughed.

"You'll be a pro with the cooktop in no time. How's Jazzy?"

"Her royal highness settled in brilliantly. Acting like she owns the place already."

"And Ian?"

"I actually haven't met him yet. I'm assuming I will tomorrow. Laney is the other working student who showed me around today. She's very sweet. I think we'll get along really well. And I also met Cooper, the assistant trainer. I didn't get much of a chance to chat with him, but he seemed nice enough. Thick Irish accent though."

"Sounds like you'll be very happy there. Molly texted me and said the farm was breathtaking."

"It is. I can't wait to get out and explore it on horseback. How are you? How's Julep?"

"I'm fine, missing you of course. Julep is heartbroken. She must have gone in and out of your room fifty times already looking for you. She's been laying in the hallway whimpering. Poor thing. She thinks you've abandoned her."

"Oh, that breaks my heart. Poor girl. I miss her so much."

"And?"

Erin laughed. "And I miss you too, of course! How are the boys? Do they care that their leading lady is gone?"

"Hunter couldn't care less. Fitz seemed a little out of sorts at first, but he's fine now. You know geldings. Easy peasy."

"They are indeed."

"So what time to you start tomorrow?"

"Six-thirty. We feed and turn out. Then we start riding. There's a schedule in the tack room that lists who gets worked and when."

"When can you ride Jazzy?"

"At the end of the day when everyone else is ridden. And I get one lesson a week from Ian. I'm looking forward to those, but Laney says he's really tough. I like a good work though, and I know Jazzy has the brain for it."

"I'll miss you so much, but I'm happy you're doing this. You are fulfilling your dreams, and before you know it, you and Jazzy will be competing at Rolex! Oh wait…I mean Land Rover. I don't think I'll get used to that change."

"Me neither," Erin said with a smile. She knew she had seen Macy earlier just that day, but it felt good to catch up with her friend.

"Well, I'd better let you go so you can concentrate on your dinner. Don't burn the barn down!"

Erin set her alarm for six o'clock the following morning, and she eagerly popped out of bed as soon as it went off. Her first day of work at her new job!

She downed a bowl of cereal, brushed her teeth, pulled her hair back into a long braid, and dressed for the day. She figured she'd be riding for most of the day, so she pulled on some breeches but grabbed her muck boots instead of paddock boots as she would be taking horses outside and walking through the mud. She'd come back for her paddock boots later when it was time to tack up.

Erin zipped up her coat, grabbed a bottle of water, and was on her way.

Both Laney and Cooper were already in the feed room.

"Coffee's brewing," Cooper said by way of greeting. "If you could feed the horses in the old barn, that would be great."

The old barn was original to the property and was the smaller one where Jazzy was stabled.

"No problem – I'll head there now."

"Grain was prepared last night, so it's ready to go. When you're done, get tonight's grain ready. The board in the feed room details who gets what. Then you can turn out."

"Sounds good, thanks," replied Erin as she shot back out the door. She wanted to show everyone that she took her job seriously and could do it well. Gotta hustle, she thought to herself as she jogged up the hill towards the old barn.

Jazzy and the other seven horses stabled there was equal parts happy to see her and dismayed that grain wasn't already in their buckets. Where have you been, they all cried!

"Hi everyone. It's not even six-thirty yet – I'm early!"

The horses settled after grain hit their buckets, and Erin took a moment to marvel at a sound she loved so much. Contented horses chomping at their breakfast brought a smile to Erin's lips.

"Are you Erin?" Asked a voice coming from behind her. She turned to see an older, slightly shorter version of Cooper.

"Yes, I am. You must be Ian – I'm so pleased to meet you." She hurried over and shook his hand.

"We're happy to have you. I'm glad we were able to make everything work out after all these years," Ian said with a polite smile, and Erin noticed that his Irish accent was not nearly as strong as Cooper's.

"Yes, better late than never, I suppose."

"I look forward to working with you. If you need anything, please don't hesitate to ask," Ian said as he turned and headed out towards the main barn.

With that, it was time to get to work. The first few horses had finished their breakfast, and it was time to take them out to their fields.

Chapter 18

Erin's first week at Emerald Isle went by in an exhausted daze. While she was used to the physical labor that came with riding and caring for horses, she'd never taken care of and ridden so many at once. By the end of the week, Erin was so sore she could hardly walk, and she was relieved that she had the afternoon off. After taking a little nap, she called Molly.

"So, how's it all going? Regret it yet?" Molly laughed.

Erin smiled into the phone – it was good to hear her sister's voice. "Not yet, although my body wishes I'd quit and come right home. I can barely move. It's pathetic."

"You'll get used to it in no time. So spill – give me the details. How's Ian? What are the horses like?"

Erin told Molly everything. Ian was nice. He wasn't exactly the hard-ass she'd been expecting, but he wasn't a walk in the park either.

"He's an interesting sort. Like – he doesn't criticize much and makes some good suggestions, but he's not high on praise either. He can be really hard to read."

"How so?"

"So normally when we're riding – me, Laney, and Cooper – we all just do our own thing, work our horses, pay attention to ourselves. The other day Ian came through and watched us all go, and he literally said not one word almost the entire time. I figured since I was new, he'd have lots of feedback for me, but no. After I was finished and was heading out of the ring, he walked over and said, 'Ride him more with your seat and less with your hands.'" Erin paused for a moment. "Of course, I know what he means, but it would have been nice if he had elaborated a bit more. Like what had I specifically been doing to make him want to tell me that?"

"Did you ask him what he meant?"

"I couldn't. He turned away the second he said it and walked off."

"Well, I'm sure he's pleased with your riding though. If he hadn't liked what he saw, I'm sure you'd have heard about it."

"I guess so. But it's a little unnerving."

"Have you had your lesson on Jazzy yet?"

"I did, this morning actually. It went well. He thinks Jazz has lots of potential and he liked her work-horse mentality. But again, he didn't say much. I flatted around to warm up while he set up a course. He did give some feedback here and there, but still, I'm surprised by how quiet he is."

"How are the others? Laney and Cooper?"

Erin told Molly that they were easy to work with, and she really liked Laney. She was quiet as well, but once Erin got her talking, they made conversation easily. Cooper was a different story – he only spoke when he had something work-related to tell her, and that was it.

"I guess the O'Ryans come by their shyness naturally, huh?" Asked Molly.

"Men of few words, that's for sure. I'll walk into the tack room and Coop has no problem giving me an overview about one of the horses or something like that – but that's it. No chit chat, nothing. I don't think he has a problem with me or anything because he's like that with Laney too – I just think that's him. So I'm determined to make him talk to me." Erin laughed.

"Of course you are!" Molly said. This was so like her sister. "Maybe he's the strong silent type who doesn't need to fill the air around him with the sound of his own voice. There's something to be said for those who sit back quietly and observe." Molly had just described herself.

"Yes there is my little author sister. But it's not going to work here – he will talk to me whether he likes it or not."

Molly laughed. "Well good luck with that. Sounds like you'll need it."

The two continued to talk for a while as Erin filled her in on some of the horses she'd been riding. Erin rode three to four a day, not including Jazzy. Her favorite was a Thoroughbred, an ex-timber horse, Ian had brought over from Ireland.

"His name is Captain and he's a big goofball, which is okay because he's only six. He's just silly – like when I first get on, I need to give him some time to get his wiggles out. He does get down to work – he knows his job – but I also get the feeling he doesn't take anything too seriously."

"He sounds like a sweetheart. Are they all Thoroughbreds?"

"The vast majority are – and most are from Ireland. They have relatives in the industry who still live in Ireland, so they funnel the ex-racers here for Ian and Cooper to retrain for eventing. He does have some Irish Sporthorses – one of which is one of Ian's Advanced horses. They went to the Olympics together!"

"Have you ridden him yet?"

"It's a mare – Panther is her barn name – and yes. I rode her yesterday, and she is just phenomenal. She attacks the jumps – absolutely loves her job. She's exactly what I want Jazzy to be."

"Well I would be lying if I said I wasn't jealous. I bet you're having the time of your life."

"I really am. Other than dropping into bed and falling asleep at eight o'clock every night, I'm having a blast. What's the news from home? Are mom and dad still mad at me?" Erin knew they weren't mad per se; they were just surprised that she gave up her stable job to take an unpaid working student position – well, in a stable.

"Neither are mad. I think mom's more upset that you moved away – you know how she likes having her daughters within a five mile radius. And dad? Well he hasn't said anything, so my guess is he's forgotten about you." Molly laughed.

"Sounds like dad," Erin said with a smile.

"But all is well here. We miss you, of course, but three months isn't too long."

"I will be home before you know it. In the meantime, I need to go take a shower. Ian invited us up to his house tonight for pizza. Laney seemed surprised so I don't think this is something he does often."

"Maybe it's a welcome-Erin-let's-get-to-know-you sort of thing."

"Maybe – I hope I'm not put on the spot. I do want to get to know them though, so this could be good."

A few hours later Erin and Laney made their up to Ian's house together, walking along the path that led through the original barn and straight to the back of the house. When Ian opened the door, a large black Labrador jumped into Erin's arms, kissing her face as if they were long lost friends finally reunited.

"Shadow, get off!" Ian yelled as he grabbed the dog's collar and attempted to pull her down. "Off! Sorry Erin," he said, still struggling to capture the wildly-wiggling dog who was now bouncing up and down in place.

"It's okay," Erin said as she reached down to rub the dog's back and lavish her with pats. "I love labs – she reminds me of my parents' dog, Rugby."

"She sees plenty of people – I don't know why she gets so excited like this," he said, slightly out of breath from wrangling his crazy beast.

"It's because she's a Lab. They're lovebugs and they can't help themselves, right Shadow?" Erin said in a playful voice. "Isn't that right, Shadow? You just can't help yourself!"

"Alright you ferocious beast, get over here and leave the nice lady alone," came Cooper's voice as he walked in the door behind her. The dog, seeing one of her friends, left Erin immediately and launched herself into Cooper's open arms.

"And just like that, I've been thrown over," Erin laughed.

"Okay everyone inside," said Ian. "You too Shadow. Party's started and they're all here for you. Come now, girl."

The back door had opened directly into a mudroom that had that classic horse farm look and feel. Wellies, paddock and field boots lined the walls, jackets and coats hung on pegs underneath shelves that contained hats, helmets, and the odd assortment of horse brushes, leather cleaner, and horse show ribbons, now vintage and faded from the sun.

Ian led the group into the kitchen, which was also at the back of the house and overlooked the yard for the dog and the stable beyond it. The kitchen was open concept with ancient cherry wood cabinets and light-colored granite countertops. The room flowed into a dining space containing a table and six chairs, and past that was a family room with comfy looking leather couches and chairs.

While the house was clean, it had that lived-in look of a typical country house. It was a home perfect for those who lived mostly out-of-doors, close to animals and nature, who sometimes brought those elements inside with them. It had that warm appeal older houses were known for, and Erin was instantly in love.

"Your house is beautiful. Thanks so much for having us over," she said with a smile. She secretly hoped he'd give her a tour of the rest of the house. Erin loved old country homes, rich in family history and heirlooms.

"You're most welcome. And dinner is served," he said with a small laugh as he gestured to the table containing multiple pizza boxes. "I got a variety so please help yourself. Coop, could you grab some glasses for the wine? There's beer and water in the fridge as well."

After they'd all served themselves and sat down at the table, Ian held up his wine glass to make a toast. "Welcome Erin, we're glad to have you. And here's to a wonderful New Year with some great horses and times ahead. Cheers."

"Cheers!" Toasted the others as they clinked their glasses.

"Thank you so much," said Erin. "I'm happy you gave me a second chance at this position all these years later."

"It's no problem at all. Our last working student was just finishing out his three months when your email came in. It was perfect timing. So – tell us a little about yourself."

Between bites of cheese pizza, Erin gave them a quick rundown. She was born and raised in Maryland in a horse-loving family and practically learned to ride before she could walk. She grew up showing in the hunters until she was bit by the eventing bug sometime in high school.

"I competed throughout high school and college, and after I graduated was when I contacted you the first time. But then I was accepted into law school and went down that path instead. I still rode, of course, but I haven't competed seriously since then." She cleared her throat and then continued. "I separated from my husband last year, well, two years ago now that it's the new year. And then last year we officially divorced. But during the separation was when I got Jazzy and decided to go full steam ahead with my riding again."

"Sorry to hear about the divorce, but we're certainly very happy you found your way back to horses," said Ian.

The spotlight was off Erin after that, and the four of them chatted easily throughout the rest of the meal. Laney, Erin learned, was from southern Virginia and had been riding for the majority of her life as well.

"I was that barn rat who worked off her lessons. My parents divorced when I was only two, and my dad moved out of state. My mom worked so hard to just make ends meet that there wasn't any money left over for riding lessons. But, luckily, there was a stable just down the street from our house – I got the bus to drop me off there after school every day so I could work off my rides."

Erin also learned that both Ian and Cooper were born in Ireland, but Ian came over to the United States in his late teen years and stayed.

"My entire family, parents, aunts, uncles, cousins, you name it, is in the horse business. Mostly flat and timber-racing – but my parents were the eventers. They came over here years ago to see what life was like in the U.S. I was eighteen or nineteen at the time. I thought of staying behind in Ireland where all my friends were but decided to tag along and help them set up shop, as they say. And well, here I am some thirty years later."

Ian's parents had purchased this farm many years ago, but sadly, his father had passed away five years ago, and his mom had died just last year.

"I thought about moving back to Ireland after mom passed, but I don't know. I don't think I could leave this farm. It was their dream and our home for years. I've lived here longer than I lived in Ireland. And, of course, it helps to have some family here," he said as he smiled over at Cooper.

"That's right – you two are cousins. How long have you been here?" Erin asked Cooper.

"Just about two years now, but I do have plans on returning to Ireland later this year. As much as I like Virginia, I just wanted to get a little experience and learn the eventing circuit here, but my goal has always been to return home."

"Of course I'm going to try and talk him into staying," Ian laughed, "but I don't blame him for wanting to go home either."

After dinner, Ian pulled out some poker chips for a rousing game of Texas Hold'em. Erin already knew how to play thanks to many poker games with Kevin and their old group of friends who enjoyed a little gambling, but Laney didn't, so they took it slow to show her the ropes.

It wasn't long before Laney caught on and won her first hand. "Well it looks like I'm in the wrong place. Forget horses. Forget eventing. I'm packing up and heading to Vegas to be a poker star!" Laney said as they all laughed.

The next hand, Erin looked at her two cards to see pocket Queens. She raised. Ian and Laney immediately folded, leaving Cooper still in who called her raise.

Out came the flop – the first three cards – and it

was another a King, a Queen, and a nine. Erin now had three of a kind with her Queens. She bet and Cooper instantly called, his stone cold face giving nothing away.

Erin watched him for a moment. "You have quite the poker face," she teased. "You don't give anything away, do you?"

"Sure don't," Cooper said seriously, but then he locked eyes with Erin and gave her a small wink.

The next card, the turn, came out – it was another King. Now Erin had a full house – Queens over Kings. This was getting interesting. She was first to act, but wanting to learn more about Cooper's hand, she only checked.

He studied her for a moment and checked as well meaning no bets were on the table but both were still in the hand. Interesting, Erin thought. Is he bluffing, she thought?

The final card, the river, came out – a three, which Erin assumed didn't help Cooper. She decided to bet the minimum amount and see how Cooper decided to act. He thought for a moment, debating to either call the current bet or raise. In the end, he just called it.

They both laid down their cards. Erin had a full house, and Cooper had an Ace and a King, which made his final hand three Kings with an Ace kicker. It was a good hand, but Erin's was better.

"Ha – got it!" Squealed Erin.

"Nice hand," said Coop with a shy smile. "I was afraid you had the full house, but when you didn't bet after the turn, it threw me off a bit."

"That was the plan," she said with a wicked smile.

"I didn't know we had a card shark in our midst," laughed Ian.

"I guess I'm going to be quitting with Laney and moving to Vegas as well," Erin said as she collected her chips.

"Nice hand, lass," Coop said again, his eyes soft and light. "I'll make a note not to underestimate you from now on."

Chapter 19

The temperatures plunged by mid-January, and snow showers fell every few days. While the accumulation didn't add up to more than a few inches here and there, it created a bit more work for everyone. Sidewalks had to be shoveled and paths to and from the fields needed to be plowed so the horses could be led in and out without incident. If it was especially icy out, then the horses just stayed in all day.

Of course Erin preferred warmer weather, but she didn't mind the cold. She thought the snow was pretty and was glad to live and work in an area that experienced all four seasons so evenly. She knew she would tire of the cold by early March, but for now the snow and sleet was expected, so she bundled up and went about her chores without thinking much about it.

She had settled into a nice routine with the rest of the staff. She rode three or four horses a day, sometimes more depending on everyone's schedules, and she usually worked Jazzy five days a week. Erin had a standing lesson with Ian on Friday mornings, and her second one had gone much better than the first with Ian giving a bit more instruction and feedback during their time in the ring. Jazzy had also settled into life at Emerald Isle Farm and happily got down to work as well.

While Erin's first impressions of everyone – that they were a quiet, almost too serious bunch – proved to be true, she realized that everyone was friendly, just focused. And once she got them talking, she was able to bring them out of their shells a bit more. Laney was her favorite, of course, as the two spent most of their time together. In the evenings they sometimes even made dinner together. It was nice to have someone to wind down the day with, talk about what had happened, ask for suggestions and feedback on one's riding, that sort of thing.

Cooper had opened up a bit more, but he was still a mystery to Erin. Most of the time he went about his business, not ignoring her per se, but not appearing approachable. But then out of nowhere he'd turn toward her and smile or give a wink as he walked past. He was a tough one to read.

It was a blustery Thursday afternoon when Erin found Laney in the tack room, cleaning the saddle she'd just ridden in.

"You finished with your rides?" Laney asked.

"Yep, all done. You?"

"I am," Laney said as she gave the saddle one last wipe and put it back on its rack. "I'm heading to Horse Country to grab some new half chaps. Want to come with?"

"I'd love to. I haven't been there in years. I need a new pair of show gloves myself, so I'll grab them while we're there."

"Great! I just saw Coop walk by. I'll see if he wants to join us," she said as she headed for the door. Erin followed.

"Hey Coop, Erin and I are heading to Horse Country for a few things. Want to tag along?"

Cooper thought for a moment before responding. "Yeah, sure, I'll come. I can always find something I need there."

"And things you don't need too," Laney laughed. "Horse Country should be renamed Horse Heaven. I always go there thinking I'm going to grab just *one* thing, and then I walk out with bags full." She shrugged. "Sometimes you just can't help splurging on some good horse stuff!"

"Give me a minute and then I'll be ready. I'll drive if you'd like."

"Sounds good."

Erin found herself secretly happy that Cooper had joined them. Maybe she could get him to open up a bit more. Being confined together in a car, even if only for a short time, was a good way to get to know someone.

"So how are you getting on?" Cooper asked Erin, who was riding shotgun in the front seat.

"Great! I love it here. I know this may sound silly, but I'm having the time of my life. The first week was rough, physically, because my body just wasn't used to riding more than one horse a day, but I'm fine now."

"Glad to hear it. And no, that doesn't sound silly. It might to others, but not to horse people," said Cooper.

"How long did you say you've been in Virginia?"

"I came over about two years ago, but I can't wait to get back. Don't get me wrong, I really like it here. I can see why Ian's chosen to make a life here, but Ireland's my home. Have you ever been?"

"I haven't. I've always wanted to visit but have never been."

"You'd love it. Some of the yards here on the east coast remind me of it, so if you like it here, you'd love it there. Come for a visit. You can always stay with me, lass," he said with an easy smile.

"Don't say that if you don't mean it because I will absolutely take you up on it! I have nothing holding me down anymore. The world is my oyster, as they say."

"Oh I mean it. I'd love to have visitors." He glanced in the rearview mirror. "That invitation goes for you too, Laney. You all are always welcome."

Before they knew it, they were heading into the little town of Warrenton, home of Horse Country Saddlery, a shop that truly had everything an equestrian could ever want – show and hunt apparel, tack, home décor, even rare and antique books – and it was all under one roof.

"I'm so excited," said Erin as she got out of the car. "I haven't been here since I was in college. I just remember spending hours here with my mom and sister."

"Well the store has expanded since then," noted Laney, "but not much else has changed. You can still spend hours on end in here and not know where the time went!"

"We're lucky we only live about twenty minutes away," said Cooper as he held the door to the store open for both ladies.

Erin stepped inside an equestrian's paradise. The large black and white tiles beckoned the group into a treasure trove of English equestrian décor, books, apparel – and each vignette displayed its own theme within.

Sitting in a zebra print chair just off center of the entrance was a middle-aged woman wearing the most endearing smile. She got up as soon as she recognized Laney.

"Laney! So good to see you," Marion exclaimed as she wrapped the girl in a tight hug.

"Marion! I was hoping you'd be here! I'd like you to meet my colleagues. Marion, this is Cooper O'Ryan and Erin Sorrenson. We all work together at Ian's farm. Guys, this is Marion Maggiolo, the owner of this amazing establishment."

"Hello and welcome," smiled Marion as she hugged each of them. "You look familiar," she said to

Cooper. "I know I've seen you here before."

"That's correct. I love it here and can't stay away for too long."

"It's nice to finally put a name with the face. But you – I don't think I've seen you before, but I could be wrong," Marion addressed Erin.

"You're right. I'm a newcomer, mostly. I visited here years ago with my mom and sister, but the last time I set foot in here was when I was in college."

"Well it's great to have you back then! Anything I can help you all with?"

"I'm here for some half chaps, but I know where they are," mentioned Laney. "But I think we're all just going to browse around for…ever!" she laughed.

"Wonderful to hear! If you need me, I'll be around. And, of course, we have multiple associates out on the floor too. Don't hesitate to give us a shout!"

With that Marion made her way toward the side of the shop that housed some offices and storage.

"She's amazing," said Laney. "I love when she's here. She adds such a brightness to the store that I just can't explain."

"What a lovely lady," smiled Erin. She turned around to address Cooper, but he had already disappeared.

"Looks like we lost Coop already. I'm going to start over here on the right and then work my way around," said Erin as she motioned towards the section displaying houseware items.

"Sounds good. I'm going to check out the half chaps first, then I'm heading downstairs to look at some of the saddles."

The girls went their separate ways, eager to check out all the treasures on each shelf and around every corner. They were sure they'd pass Cooper somewhere during their travels.

Immediately Erin spotted multiple items she wanted, but since she didn't have a house to decorate, she decided to put them on her wish list and come back another time. Another time when life was more settled and she had a place to call her own.

When she came to the gloves section, she tried on a couple of pairs but ended up choosing one of her favorite brands, SSG. They fit her long, slim fingers perfectly yet would be light and cool when showing in the summer heat. The last time she had worn her old pair, she noticed a few tears. It was time to replace them.

Erin then spent the majority of her time in the book section as they had a wide-variety of genres. From fiction and mystery to how-to and décor, Laney wasn't kidding when she said Horse Country had it all. Behind a counter were some rare books, and Erin knew that Molly would be in her glory right now if she were here.

Downstairs Erin found Coop toying with some bridles. She was about to approach but decided to hang back and study him for a moment. He was a hard one to get a handle on. Sometimes, like on the drive down, he was friendly and chatty. Other times he'd brush past Erin without so much as a glance in her direction. Was he moody? Or was he just super focused on his tasks at hand? Either way, Erin had to admit that he was rather cute. She didn't normally go for redheads, (humans, that is – she loved equine redheads), but his brilliant mane suited him. His complexion was fair as expected, but he wasn't ghostly white. And even though he could be standoffish, his green eyes were kind.

After observing him for another minute, she realized she probably looked like a stalker. *What are you doing*, she asked herself as she made her way back upstairs to find Laney.

Just over an hour later they were back on the road heading home. Erin had purchased her gloves, Laney her half chaps, and Cooper ended up grabbing a new bridle for Lucy. It had been a successful shopping trip to Horse Country, and Erin feared for her wallet as she knew there would be many more visits before her time in Virginia was up.

Chapter 20

By February's arrival, Erin had hit her stride at Emerald Isle Farm. She had developed a rhythm with her co-workers, the horses, Ian, and Jazzy, and she woke up ready to go each morning. Ian had proved to be as excellent a trainer as she had hoped, and she and Jazzy were improving with every lesson.

During one unseasonably warm, dry week in mid-February, they were all able to head out on Ian's cross country course to give all the horses a chance to really stretch their legs and take some hardier jumps. Erin couldn't keep the smile off her face as she soared over a log jump, flew down a slight bank, hopped into some shallow water, and charged up and over another log jump on the opposite side. This is it, she thought to herself. This is what I'm meant to be doing with my life. Forget law and forget the firm. I've found myself.

Not every day was perfect, of course, as working with animals as unpredictable as horses definitely had its challenges. One afternoon during "the warm up," as they were calling this reprieve from Old Man Winter's nasty grasp, Erin was taking Captain through the small water jump when he slipped badly, sending Erin sailing over his head and landing with a thud at the base of a log jump.

Cooper, on another horse, rode over quickly. "You okay?" he asked as he reached out to grab a stunned Cap who was just standing there, too confused to take off.

Erin, soaked through and through and covered with mud, laughed at herself.

"I'm okay," she said as she made her way over to Cap and gave him a thorough check for injuries. "It's been quite a while since I took a spill. Guess I was due."

Cooper dismounted alongside Erin and ran his hands down Cap's legs. "Take him over there and jog him back toward me."

Erin did as she was told and was happy to see that Cap was no worse for the wear.

"He looks good," noted Cooper as he watched the horse move with his trained eye. "Mount back up and run him through again. I saw the whole thing. I know it wasn't his fault – he just slipped – but we don't want him having any bad memories of the water. Run him through two or three more times, and then you need to go and get out of those wet clothes."

"Yes sir," smiled Erin. She took Captain far enough away to have a clean approach, asked for the canter, and sailed through the combination without a hitch. After the third clean round, she called it a day.

"Nice job," called Cooper as he flashed her a thumbs up. "Now go change!"

When Erin walked into the tack room a few hours later, she found Laney portioning the horses' evening grain.

"Heard you took a spill," she said as she scooped grain into a bucket and reached for the Cosequin supplement. "You okay?"

"Yeah, I'm fine. Already starting to stiffen up though. I just took two Advil, so hopefully those will kick in. Poor Cap. He didn't know what happened. One minute we were rolling through, and the next I was on the ground in the water."

"Coop said he slipped, poor guy."

"He did. It wasn't his fault. But I was glad Coop was there to check out Captain and make sure he was okay. It's always nice to have a second set of eyes on you."

"That it is," Laney said as she stacked the buckets up on her cart, ready to wheel it out to the horses. "Let me know if you need anything. My suggestion would be to have a nice, hot soak in the tub, but since our rooms only have showers, that's not an option," she smiled. "I do have a heating pad if you'd like to borrow it."

"Thanks, I may take you up on that."

As Erin made her way to the smaller barn to get grain ready for the horses she was in charge of, she wondered if she'd have any bruises from her fall. Not that she could do anything about it – these things happened. But she did land pretty hard at the base of the log. The life of an eventer, she thought to herself. It's a tough life, but it's a good one.

Later that evening Erin was on the phone with her mom when there was a knock at the door.

"Hey mom, let me call you back in a bit. Someone's at the door."

"No problem dear. Hope you feel better," Karen wished before they hung up.

Erin, dressed in sweats with her hair piled high on her head, padded in her slippers to answer the door. A quick look through the peephole revealed Cooper on the other side.

"Hey, Coop," she said as she opened the door and invited him in. "What brings you by?"

"I was finishing up with night check on the horses and thought I'd do a quick night check on you. See how you were feeling."

Erin gave him a smile. It was sweet that he had thought of her. "I'm starting to feel like I was hit by a bus, but I guess that's to be expected, right?"

"Have you taken anything?"

"Yes, I took some Advil earlier and was just about to take another round. I was also about to make some tea – would you like some?"

"Yes, but I'll make it. Go sit down and put your feet up."

Erin tried to protest but before she could say anything, Cooper was heading for the kitchenette.

"Love what you've done with the place, by the way," he said with a smirk. Other than a couple books on the coffee table and two framed photos – all things that Macy had sent down last month – the room was basically empty.

Erin couldn't help but laugh. "I figured no need to get settled if I'm only here for three months."

"I don't blame you. Although Ian likes you – I bet he asks you to stay on after your contract is up." Cooper set a kettle on the stove and laid out two mugs on the counter. "Sugar or honey?" He asked.

"Honey. There's some in the cabinet to the right of the microwave. Sugar's in there too if you want that."

"Honey's good for me too."

"So, do you really think Ian will extend my contract?" When she and Ian had originally discussed her position, it was a three month contract with the option to extend month-by-month after that.

"I do. He doesn't have anyone else lined up, at least not that I know of, so I would assume he'd ask you to stay. I know he likes how you ride the horses, says you've got a good way of going."

Erin beamed. "Really? I wasn't sure of his thoughts. He's awfully quiet sometimes."

"That's just Ian."

"You're awfully quiet too," Erin shot back with a

sly grin.

"That's just me." Cooper grinned right back. He walked over and handed her a mug of tea. He sat down on the couch next to her.

"Thanks for the tea, and thanks for coming to check on me. Sorry I look like something the cat dragged in."

"It's no problem. I was just a little worried – that was a pretty hard fall." His eyes roamed up and down her. "And I think you look cute." He looked away and blushed an immediate shade of red at the compliment he had given her.

"Why Coop, your face matches your hair," Erin laughed. She was secretly pleased at the attention he was showing her. It was unexpected, which made it even better.

Sensing she'd made Cooper uncomfortable, she changed the subject to something safer.

"When do Ian and Laney leave for the clinic?" Ian had been invited to give a multi-day Intro to Eventing clinic down in the Richmond area and had asked Laney to assist him. Even though Ian would be heading it, Laney would still have an opportunity to work with some of the students, so she was really excited.

"They leave next Thursday and won't be home until the following Monday," he answered.

"So it's just you and me holding down the fort?"

"Yep. Just you and me."

Chapter 21

The stable was a whirlwind of activity after Ian and Laney left before the sun was even up on Thursday morning. Ian didn't expect Erin and Cooper to ride all the horses that were normally assigned to himself and Laney, but of course they wanted to fit in as many as possible. Even though they would only be gone a few days, it was important to keep the horses as close to their routines as possible.

Erin barely had a moment to breathe, but she was loving every minute. This was the work she was made for. Her body was meant to be pushed and pulled, taxed to the limit by these magnificent beasts, and she'd never felt more alive. Her mind, as well, was busier than it had ever been – even during law school or in the middle of some of her toughest, most challenging cases.

Horses demanded 100% of you, your mind, your thoughts, every single ride. Erin loved their complexities, that each horse had its own quirks, its own differences that made her have to rethink her training methods and figure out which ones worked best for each animal. She felt alive for the first time in years, and even though it was the middle of winter and she was pale from lack of sun, Erin knew she had a glow about her.

She knew she was where she was supposed to be, and her phone call with Molly last night had solidified it.

After telling Erin most of the news from back home, she paused. She had gone back and forth on whether or not to tell her sister about her recent run-in with Kevin, but she decided to just go ahead and do it.

"There's also another thing I should mention," Molly hesitated.

"Uh oh, this doesn't sound good."

"I ran into Kevin at Wegmans the other day."

"In Hunt Valley? What on earth was Kevin doing out that way?" Kevin lived in Baltimore City, a good forty minutes south of Hunt Valley, which wasn't far from where the Sorrensons and Macy all lived.

"That's the thing. He told me he had just moved out here. Apparently he and his girlfriend moved in together…and she's actually his fiancé now."

For a moment Erin was speechless. This wasn't news she was expecting to hear. She knew that Kevin and Delaney had been dating for a couple months, but engaged?

"Erin?" Molly asked. "You still there?"

"Yes, sorry, I'm here. I was letting that sink in for a minute. Engaged? Already? They've been together, what, four, five months?"

"He told me six, which isn't much better, of course. But he said he was ready and so was she. And she's from the area and wanted him to move out of the city, so here he is."

"Isn't that nice. I had wanted to move out of the city for years and he'd never consider it. I guess this girl's got the magic touch."

"I almost said exactly that to him, but I didn't want to start anything. But I don't like that now we'll run into him here and there."

"Yeah, that'll make for some uncomfortable small talk in the middle of the grocery store," Erin sighed. "But what can you do? He's got to continue on with his life." As Erin said this, she was overcome with a feeling of pure relief. She was relieved that she was doing just that – continuing on with her life, and she could honestly say that she was happy.

"It's so weird though," said Molly. "I was looking

at this guy who's been a member of my family for years, but as we were talking, he just felt like a stranger. I'm sorry to spring this on you, but I thought you should know that he's in the area now…and engaged."

"Don't be sorry at all. I'm glad you told me – really. And while the news caught me by surprise, I'm okay. I didn't think he'd get engaged so fast, but…it feels okay."

"Not like a punch in the gut?"

"Not at all. I miss him, of course, but we weren't meant to be. And even though I'm still sad about how things worked out, I do want him to be happy."

As Erin placed Captain in cross-ties and began brushing his dark bay coat, she again felt relieved that Kevin had moved on. She could finally go confidently in the direction of her dreams without worrying that she'd crushed Kevin's happiness. He was okay, and so was she.

"Want to grab some dinner later?" Cooper asked as he led Lucy out of the indoor arena. His question took Erin by surprise. Even though it was just the two of them here now, they'd been so busy with their horses and barn chores they'd hardly said a word to each other.

"Sure!" she said to quickly fill the silence.

"Great! I was thinking we'd stay close and grab a bite in town. Have you been to the Front Porch yet?"

"No, not yet. I've driven by it a bunch though. Looks like a cute place."

"Yeah, we like it, great food. Let's go as soon as we're done."

"Looking forward to it," Erin said genuinely. A smile began to spread across her lips, but she quickly admonished herself. *It's just dinner, not a date!*

Two hours later, after each had finished with their horses and had time to take a quick shower, Erin and Cooper turned right out of the driveway and headed into the small town of The Plains.

The town was tiny, consisting of just a handful of shops and restaurants. They found parking behind the Front Porch Café and meandered in through their back door. The hostess up front saw them coming and pointed to a small table in the corner. Cooper let her have the booth side with its back to the windows. He took the chair opposite.

The restaurant was small but what it lacked in size it made up for in character and warmth. The place was downright cozy with its bright paint color and vibrant pictures hung on the walls.

"Thanks for suggesting this place; I've been wanting to try it," Erin said as she placed her napkin in her lap and picked up the menu.

"I figured we earned ourselves a little treat since we'll be working out tails off for the next few days."

The waiter then came over, and he filled their glasses with water as he delivered the specials of the evening. Even though they sounded wonderful, they chose items on the menu. Cooper ordered a personal pizza, and Erin went with the tomato soup for a starter and the blackened salmon for her entrée.

"Would you care for anything other than water to drink?" asked the waiter as he scribbled down their orders.

"I'd like the Devils Backbone," said Cooper, referring to a lager brewed locally in Lexington, Virginia.

"I think I'll order something local as well," Erin noted as she perused the menu a bit more. "Okay, let's try the Three Fox Calabrese Pinot Grigio."

"Excellent choice," smiled the waiter. "I'll be back with your drinks in just a moment."

Their orders placed, Erin took a deep breath and exhaled loudly as she slouched back against the booth. "I'm beat."

"Really makes you appreciate when we're full-staffed, right? You don't realize how everyone pulls their own weight until they're gone. Thank goodness Paul is still here." Knowing that they were short-staffed, Paul would pick up a few additional hours to help lighten Cooper and Erin's load. Every little bit helped when you were caring for and riding an entire stable full of horses.

"So tell me the truth," Cooper continued. "Are you enjoying yourself here? Or are you homesick for your old life."

Erin laughed at that. "Definitely not homesick. Instead of sitting in an office for hours every day and being surrounded by angry people who absolutely hate their soon-to-be ex-significant others, I am training and riding some of the best horses I will ever get to sit astride."

"Pretty happy then, huh?" Cooper smiled. He was glad that Erin had acclimated well. Prior to her joining them, Ian had told him that she was leaving her job at the law firm and looking for something new. While he understood the need for change, sometimes too much change too quickly backfired.

"I was definitely skeptical when I got here. While I knew in my heart that I was done with law, of course you never really know how you're going to feel about something until you're in the middle of it. But here I am, and I'm loving life."

"Do you miss your ex?"

"You know it's funny. Last night I was chatting with my sister, and she told me she ran into my ex at the grocery store. And get this – he's engaged already. I was surprised when she told me, but it wasn't the punch in the gut I expected. My only issue now is that he's moved closer to my hometown, so chances of running into him are higher. But it is what it is. I'll always love him, just not like I used to."

"Sounds like you made the right decision then, coming here."

"I did. It was a spur of the moment thing, emailing Ian a couple months ago, but it was meant to be." Erin paused as she took a sip of the wine the waiter had just set down. "Mm…delicious. What about you? Any leading ladies in your life?" Erin was someone who always got right to the point.

"Besides some of my favorite fillies and mares, not a one. I had a girl back home, but things were beginning to fizzle just before I moved here. We officially pulled the plug before I left Ireland. We knew a long-distance thing wouldn't work. Hell, a short-distance thing wasn't working," he laughed.

"And you haven't met anyone here?"

"I've had a few dates here and there, but no one has really turned my head, so to speak. Besides, I'm too busy to date…and I'm leaving to go back home in a few months, so it wouldn't really make sense." Erin couldn't help but notice the tinge of sadness in his eyes as he said that. He looked at her and gave her a wistful smile.

"Any chance you'd stick around a little longer?"

Cooper hesitated a bit and again held eye contact with Erin for a few beats longer than expected. "I've thought about it, and I know Ian would love it, but it's time to head back and be with my family. I won't lie though, I'll miss it here. Virginia's lovely, and Ian's built a brilliant life for himself."

"But you'll come back and visit?"

"Wild horses couldn't keep me away."

They drove home from dinner in silence. Not an awkward silence, but the comfortable kind where you don't need to say anything in order to enjoy the other person's company. Their food had been delicious, and the conversation had been easy and fun. Cooper can be so reserved at times that Erin wasn't sure how the evening was going to go, but they had an easy banter with, at least on her end, an undercurrent of flirtation and lust. There was something about this Irish lad that stirred something inside of Erin – something she hadn't felt in years since she first met Kevin. *Maybe I'm just attracted to guys I can't have. In just a few months, we'll be separated by the Atlantic Ocean. Definitely not one to get involved with.*

Unless this was just what she needed. What better rebound than with someone who wasn't sticking around anyway?

When they arrived back at the farm, they walked down the aisles of the barns doing night check together. Everyone was all accounted for, snoozing softly, with buckets full of water and nets full of hay.

Cooper headed towards the stairs to the apartments and offered his arm. "Allow me to see you back to your place, las?"

"Why thank you kind sir," she smiled, happily taking his arm.

When they stopped on the landing right outside her door, she fished in her purse for her key. "Would you like to come in for a night cap? And by that, I mean either coffee or tea."

Cooper hesitated and bit his lip, clearly trying to decide what to do. "Maybe some other time," he said, disappointment in his eyes. "I had a very nice evening, thanks for joining me."

Erin, trying to hide the displeasure in her own eyes, thanked him for inviting her. "Have a good night. I'll see you bright and early tomorrow."

With that Cooper began to lean in to kiss her, but for some reason stopped himself. Instead, he reached over, tucked a stray strand of hair behind Erin's ear, and whispered, "See you tomorrow." And before he could change his mind, and before Erin could stop him, Cooper turned on his heel and headed back down the stairs.

Chapter 22

After Cooper's departure, Erin changed into her pajamas and got ready for bed. *He was going to kiss me,* she thought. *I just know it…but what stopped him?*

Maybe he doesn't want to get involved with a co-worker, she figured as she placed the tea kettle on the stove to heat some water for tea. She pulled down the honey and grabbed a spoon from the drawer. As she waited for the water to boil, Erin realized that she felt restless…and sad.

It had been a long time since she'd felt desired in the way Cooper had made her feel tonight. Sure, she knew that Leo was attracted to her, and she to him if she were being honest with herself, but there was something about Cooper. Maybe he was just the forbidden fruit. After all, she would only be working here a little while longer, and then Cooper was going back to Ireland. It made no sense to get involved with someone who was going to be so unavailable, but Erin couldn't deny that she was drawn to him in a way she hadn't been since Kevin.

The kettle started to whistle, so she pulled if off the stove and poured herself a large cup. After she stirred in some honey, she walked over to her window, the mug warm between her hands. From her view out of the window, she could see Cooper's small house off to the right. It sat behind Ian's house but off to the side and surrounded by trees. Very private. Even if he were home, there's no way Ian could see the comings and goings of Cooper's house.

Laney's apartment right next door had the same view as Erin's, but she wasn't home either.

Before she could do something she'd regret, Erin finished her tea and got in bed. It was just after ten o'clock and even though she was wide awake, she knew she'd better force herself to go to sleep.

After almost an hour of tossing and turning, Erin gave up. She got out of bed and padded over to the couch where she'd sit and read until sleep finally came. As she walked over to the couch, she glanced out the window again – she couldn't help herself – and saw with delight that Cooper's lights were still on. He was awake too, unusual for someone who got up at the crack of dawn every morning.

Oh to hell with it, Erin thought. *You only live once.*

And with that last thought, she quickly changed out of her pajamas into jeans and a sweatshirt, and out the door into the night she went.

Even though there wasn't anyone around to see her, she carefully crept down the stairs and into the main barn. She waited a moment for her eyes to adjust to the darkness before continuing on her journey to Cooper's house. She stealthily stole through the night, wandering along the shadows' edges on her way to her destination. Should she go to the front door or around the back?

Since no one was home on the farm except for them, Erin went to the front door, sneaking up quietly like a cat just in case she changed her mind at the last second.

The curtain to the window to the right of the door was open, and Erin could see Cooper inside, sitting on the couch. She could hear the buzzing from the TV, but Cooper was sitting forward with his elbows on his knees, head in his hands, not watching.

Here goes nothing.

She knocked on the door and saw Cooper jump

off the couch. The front porch lights were off, so he wouldn't be able to see who was at the door until he answered it.

Without asking who was there, Cooper swung the door open and Erin would later swear that his face went from displaying a mask of confusion to one of pure, utter joy.

Before she could say a word, Cooper reached out and pulled Erin to him in a strong, passionate kiss. He held her in his embrace for a few moments before pulling away. "Please tell me this is why you're here, lass," he said as he cradled Erin's head in his hands.

She nodded. "Yes," she answered and then leaned into his kiss again. It was hungry and raw, and it was just a matter of seconds before Cooper led her inside and scooped Erin up in his well-muscled arms. He carried her back to his bedroom and laid her on his bed.

"I can't believe you're here," he said as he began to undress her. "I was thinking of coming back to you, but I didn't see your light on."

"I tried to go to bed," Erin said as she pulled Cooper's shirt off over his head. "But I couldn't sleep."

Now both fully naked, Cooper began to explore Erin's body with his mouth, kissing every inch of her skin. He took her breast in his mouth and sucked while Erin arched her back, relishing his touch. But she couldn't wait much longer. "Please, I need you," she whispered as she grabbed at him down below.

"Your wish is my command," he smiled. "But I just realized I don't have any protection."

"I'm on the pill, and I haven't been with anyone since my ex. I'm good without a condom if you are."

"Same here. It's been quite some time for me too," said Cooper as he began to kiss her again while reaching down and sliding a finger inside her. She was ready for him.

He drove her crazy for a few moments, squirming under his tender touch, but then Erin reached down and grabbed him. She lifted her hips to meet him, and he swiftly slid inside until they were one.

As they moved together, arms and legs intertwined, holding each other tightly, Erin felt herself falling for this man. Cooper held her so tenderly, yet his passion was powerful. Moving with him, she no longer felt broken or unwanted. She no longer felt like an outcast in society, like someone who just didn't fit. Erin felt, for the first time in a long time, like she belonged. It was more than just sex, and Erin wished she could read Cooper's mind to see if he felt the same connection she did.

It wasn't long before they both climaxed and collapsed into each other's arms, spent yet happy and glowing.

As Cooper rolled to his side, he wrapped his arms around Erin and pulled her close to him. "Stay with me tonight," he whispered into her ear. And since no one would know the wiser, she did.

Chapter 23

And so it began. Almost every night, late after she was sure Laney had fallen asleep in her apartment next door, Erin would look outside to see Cooper's light on. And that was their sign, the all-clear. She'd slowly sneak down the stairs, across the back lawn, and into Cooper's waiting arms. Night after night they'd make love, and little by little Erin would leave a piece of her heart with him afterwards when she'd make her way back to her room a few hours before the world awakened.

Of course Erin told Molly and Macy about her little tryst, but she was afraid to say anything to Laney for fear of word getting out and getting into trouble with Ian. Not that she'd get fired, or at least she didn't think she would, but she and Cooper both agreed to keep up the professional front. It would just be their little secret. Which, Erin acknowledged to herself, made it even sexier.

"And so you meet him every night?" Asked Macy one evening after Erin called to chat.

"Not every night…but most."

"You must be exhausted."

Erin gave a dry laugh. "You have no idea. And I have to sneak back every night. I don't want anyone catching me doing the walk of shame."

"Why can't he come to you?"

"Laney would hear. These walls are paper thin."

"So you're a screamer, huh?" Macy couldn't help herself.

"You are terrible! But even if we were super quiet, there's still a chance she'd hear him coming and going, and we don't want anyone finding out."

"Did you ever read that Danielle Steel novel, *Palomino*?"

Erin thought for a second. "I think so…refresh my memory."

"I can't remember their names, but the main character takes a break from her big city life and job to go work on a friend's ranch out west. She falls for the head honcho cowboy and ends up sneaking into his cabin every night. I think she climbs out her window and shimmies down from the second story."

"I remember now!"

"Well that's you! You're Palomino!"

Erin doubled over with laughter. "Good lord – life imitates art. I hope Molly doesn't end up writing a book about my disastrous life."

"Your life isn't a disaster – it's exciting! The divorce, the new job…just think of it all as a plot twist. A new chapter."

"You're turning into Molly with your analogies, you know. But I love it."

"I think we've all merged into one person at this point. So, how's work going?"

"Great! I actually have my first show coming up. It's a schooling show not too far from here. I'm taking Jazzy and Captain. It'll be nice and low key for all the horses – Laney and Coop are showing too. Ian will just be there to coach us."

"That sounds fun! Will you be going to any full-blown events?"

"I think so, but nothing's set yet. I have to get Jazzy out on cross country a bit more before I'm comfortable competing in a full event. She's been handling everything in stride though, so it won't be long now."

Macy paused for a moment. "I'm so happy you

did this, you know. Left your job and followed your heart. I haven't heard you sounding this happy in, well, years really. I know you're enjoying your time with Cooper, but it's the job and the horses that are bringing you back to life."

"Thanks for saying that. It's true – I feel better than I have in ages. Happier, lighter – like my life is going exactly as it should be. I appreciate you telling me. I've been thinking that myself, but it's nice to hear it from someone else. I second guessed every single decision I've made in the last two years, but I finally feel free. Like I made it to the other side and life looks pretty good from where I'm sitting."

"It looks pretty great from where I'm sitting too. I'm proud of you, my friend."

Macy's call bolstered up Erin even more. For the first time in longer than she could remember, she felt ready for anything – like she could do or be anything she wanted. She felt a certain optimism and enlightenment that she hadn't felt since she was a child.

Youth gives you that carefree feeling – that your life is laid out before you and you can head in any direction you please. But then reality kicks in and adulthood comes flying at you, and before you know it, you can't think about anything other than your responsibilities and obligations. Real life sneaks up on you and takes your dreams, in that childhood sense, away. And the farther you get from them, the harder it is to remember what they were to begin with.

But not now. Now Erin was back in the driver's seat, taking control of the wheel, and steering her life exactly where she wanted it to go.

Cooper was definitely an added, and unexpected,

complication on her road to recovery. She really hadn't wanted to start a relationship with anyone so soon after her divorce, but she couldn't help herself with Cooper. And who knows what they really were – they hadn't talked about their relationship in that capacity yet. And Erin didn't want to. She was completely content with their situation at the moment. They'd figure things out eventually. Or maybe they wouldn't. But all Erin knew was that life was looking pretty peachy, and she couldn't wait to see what the next chapter had in store.

Chapter 24

Horse show mornings aren't for the faint of heart. Up and at 'em hours before the sun comes up, there are horses to bathe, tack to clean, and trailers to pack. Of course, some of this can be done the day before, but there is always that last minute checking and double checking to make sure an all-important piece of equipment or apparel isn't left behind.

Today's event was a jumper schooling show at a nearby farm, and Erin was a little apprehensive because she and Jazzy were making a big jump in levels with the .00 m which was 3'3". They'd been schooling three feet at home for weeks now, and Jazzy was breezing through her lines and grids, so Erin felt they'd make a strong showing in the competition today with their three rounds.

She'd also be showing Captain, and since it was his first ever horse show, they'd compete in the .70m which was 2'3". If Erin could keep his mind focused, she knew they'd deliver some great performances. While Cap lacked Jazzy's all-business attitude, he did give his all if Erin kept his mind from wandering. A horse who needed constant stimulation, Cap was a challenge, but Erin felt they were ready for the show.

Since it was a schooling show and early March, the dress was casual, so Erin would be wearing breeches, field boots, a long-sleeved Under Armour shirt with an Essex Classics sweater layered on top. She had an Ariat vest that she could throw on if it was extra cold in the farm's indoor arena.

She had loaded most of her gear into the tack/dressing room of the five-horse trailer the night before, but she did one last check that she had everything she'd need. Erin then brought over her grooming supplies and brush caddy. Now it was time to load up the horses.

Laney was riding her horse, Jester, and Cooper was riding his mare, Lucy, along with one of Ian's newer horses, River. Ian would be coming along as well, but only as their coach and not as a competitor himself. Erin was looking forward to having Ian watch her rides and give feedback throughout the day. He always seemed to know what little issues she was having without her telling him and would proactively offer advice that hit the spot. He was a true horseman, and Erin still felt a little intimidated by him.

The drive to the show grounds only took about twenty minutes, and it was immediately evident as soon as they pulled in to park that they weren't the only ones hoping to get a jumpstart on the spring show season. The field used for parking was already crowded, and horses and riders were everywhere. This should have made Erin nervous, but it only added to her excitement. She'd traded courtrooms for riding rings. Not an attorney in sight – these were her people, and this was how she should be spending her Saturday.

"I'll stay here and keep an eye on things," said Ian as he got out of the driver's seat. "You three go register and get your numbers."

"You ready for your big debut?" Cooper asked Erin as they walked with Laney to the barn where a little registration tent was set up.

"Debut?"

"Yes, your first show as a member of the Emerald Isle team," he said with a smile.

"Oh! Yes, absolutely. I just hope I get around without embarrassing you all. It's one thing to show by yourself and not care if you mess up, but it's another when you're representing Ian O'Ryan," she said in a serious tone.

"Well get that out of your mind right now, lass. Ian will be happy as long as you give it your all and give the horses their best chance out there. He doesn't expect all blue ribbons. He does expect hard work and improvement though. But I've seen you ride enough to know how serious you take this sport."

"Besides," Laney piped up. "You and Jazzy have been going beautifully. You'll dominate today."

"And Captain?" Erin asked with a smile. The gelding was getting a reputation for being a challenge. Both Laney and Cooper had ridden him, but neither had as much success as Erin in getting him to get down to work.

"For you? He'll jump the moon. For me or Coop? He might not make it over the first fence," Laney smirked.

The three of them laughed because it was kind of true. Laney had ridden Cap the other day and for no reason whatsoever, the horse refused the first fence of the course Laney had wanted to jump. When he realized how upset his refusal made his rider, Captain thought it would be fun to refuse again. Erin was in the ring on Jazzy and could swear that Captain's expression was one of pure amusement.

Laney eventually got him around the course; it wasn't pretty, but they did it. Afterward as she was untacking, she loudly proclaimed, "Erin, this horse is ALL YOURS from here on out!"

It was obvious that Cap had bonded with Erin and that she was his person. All things considered, Laney was definitely the more experienced rider of the two, but Erin had that something special as far as the horse was concerned.

"Everyone's going to kill it today. I just know it,"

said Cooper after they got their numbers and made their way back to the trailer.

Upon arrival they were greeted by two very familiar faces – Molly and Macy!

"You guys made it!" Erin cried as she ran up to greet her sister and best friend.

"Of course! We wouldn't miss it!" They cried as Erin pulled them both into a three-way hug. She hadn't seen either since she moved in January and seeing both here right now made Erin realize how much she'd missed them.

"I like them already," laughed Ian. "They brought food!" He pointed over to the trailer where laid out on the floor of the dressing room were doughnuts, coffee, a fruit platter, and some breakfast sandwiches.

"Can't very well show on an empty stomach," Molly said. They'd picked everything up at a bakery not too far away.

"Thank you so much – I'm starving," said Erin as she made a beeline for a breakfast sandwich.

After everyone had eaten their fill and said their thanks to Macy and Molly for their generosity, it was time to unload the horses and get to work.

There were five horses between three riders, so having Macy and Molly on hand was a huge help. Molly took Jazzy so Erin could concentrate on getting Captain ready. Since he was jumping the lowest, his classes would be first.

Despite the show's crowds and buzzing atmosphere, all of the horses remained relatively calm as they were brought out, groomed, and tacked up for schooling. Captain was a little strong in his warm-up, but he was responsive and listening to Erin. After putting him through his paces, she quickly passed him off to Macy to hold so she could take Jazzy for a spin. As usual, the mare got down to business.

After warm-up, four of the horses went back on the trailer while Captain remained tacked. His classes were due to start shortly, so Molly hand-walked him around to keep him limber. Laney volunteered to stay back at the trailer to keep an eye on everyone so the others could watch Erin's rounds. She'd be riding three back-to-back jump courses, all of which she'd already memorized. She was ready.

"You all looked fantastic!" Macy beamed as she helped Erin unload the trailer later that evening. The show had gone better than expected. Captain's classes were rather large, but they pulled out some respectable placings, especially since it was his first show. He was a bit nervous in his first class and took a rail down because he was too busy looking at the crowd and not what was in front of him. But the rail actually worked to bring him back into focus, with Erin's help of course, and they finished that course and completed the next two beautifully. They ended the day with a sixth, a third, and a second – improving with each ride. Erin was thrilled with his progress.

Jazzy was a machine. From the moment they entered the ring of their first class, she was completely focused on the task at hand. Though she was still fairly green, she knew her job and loved it. Their rounds were clean and fast, earning them two blue ribbons and one red. Erin was over the moon.

Cooper and Laney did well with their mounts too, and no one came home empty-handed. While Ian had some constructive feedback for all of them, he was very pleased with his students' performances and excited for what the spring season would bring. Erin was only sorry that she wouldn't be a part of it. Her working student contract was up at the end of the month.

"Thanks!" Erin said to Macy, grinning with pride as she hung her bridle on its peg and began to clean it. "I knew Jazzy would give it her all, but I wasn't sure what to expect from Cap. It took him that first round to figure it out, but then he brought it, didn't he?"

"He certainly did," said Molly as she hoisted a saddle onto its rack and covered it. "He looked so confused when he hit that rail, but then it's like a switch flipped and he got it."

"He's so cute too, isn't he?" Erin asked. True, with his dark chocolate brown coat and small white star, Captain was a dreamboat.

"A showstopper, that's for sure," smiled Macy. "Do you have time for a quick dinner with us before we head out?"

"I do."

"Invite the others too, especially loverboy," Macy said with her Cheshire cat grin.

"Shh!!" Erin shushed her as she quickly turned around to make sure no one was walking in the room to overhear. "No one else knows, and we really want to keep it that way."

"I must say, you guys do a great job of hiding it. Had I not known that you were doing the dirty, I never would have guessed," said Molly.

"I don't think Coop really cares if word got out, but I don't want it to. I'm only here for a short time and I want to be seen as the ultimate professional – not that working student who shacked up with the assistant trainer."

"I'm surprised you care. The Erin I know wouldn't give a shit," Macy said with a wink.

"You know, I was thinking about that the other

day, and you're right," agreed Erin. "Normally I would go about my business, the rest of the world be damned. But…this is my new life now. I'm not just talking about my life post-divorce. I mean – horses. I want to go into the industry. I'm not sure in what capacity yet, exactly, but I know for one thing that I'm never going back to law."

"Don't tell dad," Molly laughed. She knew their father had loved bragging about the attorney in the family. Not to mention all the education and hard work Erin had put into her career – their dad just didn't want to see her give up on it so quickly.

"Yeah, this conversation never happened," Erin said. She knew she could trust her sister to keep a secret. "I have some ideas I've been rolling around in my head – some things in the works – but nothing concrete. But I'll get there. Right now, I want to give this job 110% and then figure out the next step as it comes."

"That sounds like a perfect plan, and you know we support you completely," said Macy as she finished sorting the grooming area. "We're both proud of you. You might feel like you turned your life upside down, and of course change is hard, but you did what you needed to do to put yourself and your happiness first. That takes a lot of guts."

Erin walked over and hugged her friend. "Thanks Mace. I'm so happy you guys made it down here today. I can't believe how much I've missed you two."

"Hey wait for me!" Molly cried as she came over and joined the hug. "It's not the same at home without you, but we're so happy you're here and killing it!"

"And we're also happy you've found someone to have a little…*ahem*…fun with!" Macy grinned as Erin laughed. She was pretty happy about that too.

Chapter 25

Erin stood in the aisle of the original barn as she watched Molly and Macy's taillights grow smaller. What a wonderful day it had been – successful rides at the show and a happy visit with the ones she loved most. Watching them drive away now left her with an ache she hadn't felt in years – probably not since she had gone away to college all these years ago. She missed her family, but this was where she was supposed to be.

Before she made her way back to her apartment, she stopped at Jazzy's stall.

"Knock, knock," she said quietly to the mare who was eating hay in the back of her stall. "Care for a quick visit?" Erin asked as she unlatched the door and let herself in.

Jazzy stopped munching for a moment and turned to greet her mom. In an uncharacteristic affectionate moment, she laid her head against Erin's chest while Erin scratched her horse's neck and massaged her ears.

After about a minute, Jazzy decided she'd had enough and that her hay was more interesting. Still, Erin appreciated the quiet moment with her mare. "Your bark is worse than your bite, you know that? I've got your number."

Erin gave her horse a hug, and as if to prove a point, Jazzy pinned her ears flat back but stood quietly. "See? You're all talk." Erin loved a fiery mare and was so grateful to have Jazzy in her life.

When she got back into her apartment, Erin jumped in the shower to scrub away the dirt and grime of the horse show. Thankfully, it was still early March, so the temperatures were mild, chilly even. They had climbed into the fifties today, which was pretty normal, but with her nerves and back to back rides on both horses, Erin had sweated a bit.

She got out of the shower, brushed her teeth, and pulled her wet hair back into one long braid. Today had been a good day, the kind of day you want to sit on the couch with someone and talk through, rehash all the sweet moments. Being there and experiencing it all with Molly and Macy had made it all the more sweeter – and riding alongside Cooper had been the icing on the cake. Their romance was something that had caught Erin off guard, but she had realized today that she was proud to be with him – even if only she knew. Well, Macy and Molly knew too, but besides them, their relationship was private. But today as she had watched him ride his rounds, looking handsome in his riding apparel, she had known in her heart that he was hers. And that had been enough for her.

With a smile playing on her lips, she walked to the window and looked out into the night. There, like a beacon of hope, was his porch light, beckoning her in, welcoming her. She grabbed her coat and off she went.

"Well lassie, you sure showed them today," was the first thing Cooper said when he opened the door. But instead of responding, Erin jumped into his arms and kissed him deeply.

"That's some greeting," he laughed as he pulled away long enough to close the door behind her.

"I was just thinking about you and how much I enjoyed watching you today. There's something sexy about watching someone do the one thing they do best. I guess it's the confidence."

"Well I liked watching you perform as well. I

always love it when you wear those tight breeches. Good thing for me I get to see them every single day."

And with that Cooper scooped her up into his arms and carried her into the bedroom. Maybe it was the high from the show or maybe it was the high that comes with keeping a delicious secret only you know, but Erin couldn't undress Coop fast enough.

"Slow down, lass. We have all night."

But Erin didn't slow down. She yanked off his sweatshirt and unbuckled his pants at lightning speed. Before Cooper knew what was happening, she was on her knees with him in her mouth. He couldn't speak but only groan in pleasure.

After a few moments of bliss, he pulled her up and laid her on the bed. "I can't wait any longer," he whispered as he got on top and slid inside her. Erin moaned as he fully entered her, and then began to move with him, biting his shoulder and kissing his neck.

"What's gotten into you?" He asked softly. "Maybe we should go to horse shows more often." Erin was like a wildcat, and Cooper just went along for the ride.

After they finished, Erin lay in Cooper's arms breathing heavily but smiling like the cat who ate the canary. He leaned over and kissed the side of her head. "I don't know why, but I almost feel as if I've been taken advantage of," he laughed. "But you won't hear me complaining, that's for sure."

Erin giggled. "Do you feel used? Sorry, not sure what came over me. I just had to have you. Had to be with you."

She rolled over to look Cooper directly in his eyes which were soft yet serious. "What are we going to do?"

He asked. "We've certainly got ourselves into a predicament."

"That we have," Erin agreed. "I leave at the end of the month. When are you supposed to go back to Ireland?"

"As of right now – end of May. Any chance you'd stay here until then?"

"Ian hasn't mentioned it. Does he have another student coming in?"

"Not that I know of. I'll ask him what his plans are – casually float it out there. I know you want to keep things quiet, so I'll be vague."

"If he'll have me, then I'd love to stay until then."

"Any chance you'd stay longer? Laney's been here for a while, and I don't think she has any plans on leaving. I'm sure Ian would love having you stay even longer after I leave. Make the transition easier."

"Honestly, I have no idea. I wouldn't be opposed to extending my contract a little, but I do want to head back at some point this year. Maryland is my home."

"I know what you mean," he sighed. "But that doesn't really solve *our* problem, does it?"

"Sure doesn't," Erin said softly as she rolled back over. Cooper pulled her close to him, curling himself tightly to her body.

Erin would never ask him to give up going back home to Ireland. She understood what home meant and why it was so important for him to return to his family and friends. And since their relationship – or whatever this was – was still so new, it would be too forward, too presumptuous of her to ask him to stay. They both knew that this time together wouldn't last forever, but Erin was content, at least for right now, to put it from her mind. She didn't want to put a damper on the present by worrying about the future.

Chapter 26

By the end of March, the Virginia countryside became a sight to behold. The trees began to bud, the grass started to turn green, and the temperatures warmed. There was still a ways to go before flowers would bloom, but the sun was shining, the skies were blue, and the world around them was coming back to life.

Erin started her mornings in jackets or sweatshirts, but by the afternoons, she had stripped down to short-sleeved shirts. She loved spring. The air was clean and clear, the days grew longer, the sun warmed her skin, and the dreaded humidity hadn't creeped in just yet. The earth was rejuvenating itself after a long hibernation, and Erin enjoyed every minute.

That afternoon she had schooled Captain in the outdoor jump ring. That was another thing – while she loved the access of an indoor arena and the ability to still ride in the winter when the weather turned, she kicked it to the curb the moment she could. Erin would choose riding outside in the fresh air any day over the stuffy indoor, beautiful and convenient as it was.

After flatting Cap for about twenty minutes, she started popping him over some cross-rails to warm up, first at the trot, then the canter. He was focused as he collected himself over jump after jump, and Erin found it hard to believe that this was the same horse who had bucked off Laney just two days before.

Since the horse show had gone so well, Laney decided to try her luck with the Thoroughbred again only to have him launch her to the sky halfway through their schooling session. Cap had been difficult the entire time, but Laney was an excellent rider and worked him through it the best she could. At the end of a clean line of jumps, Captain celebrated his success by sending poor Laney through the air.

Luckily, Erin and Ian were in the indoor and saw the entire thing. Ian ran over to make sure Laney was okay, (she was – just a little bruised), while Erin, on Jazzy, trotted alongside Cap until she caught his reins and ponied him back over to Laney. Ian checked Cap for any injuries, and once he gave the green light, Laney vaulted back in the saddle and was bounding down the line again before Captain knew what hit him. They came through clean without any theatrics this time. Ian made them repeat the exercise two more times, and then they called it a day.

Then yesterday Ian wanted to have a go on the horse, and while Cap didn't try anything untoward with the trainer, he certainly didn't put forth a nice ride. Captain did what was asked of him but looked absolutely bored. There was no excitement in his eyes, and the vim and vigor he reserved solely for Erin was gone. He was becoming a one-woman horse, and Ian wasn't thrilled about it.

Still, he needed to be exercised and needed consistent training, so Erin remained his regular rider. Cooper had volunteered to school Cap later in the week, and Erin was curious to see how that turned out.

After warming up over the smaller jumps, Erin dismounted to raise a handful of them, create some oxers, and pull a brush jump out into the middle of the ring. The course she laid out ranged from 2' to 2'6", and she felt confident that Cap would handle all of it with ease.

And he did. He soared over each jump with room to spare and listened to Erin's every command.

"Look at that little asshole – he's behaving like a lamb," called Laney as she walked into the ring leading

Jester. "You've definitely got the magic touch."

"I don't know what it is – I'm not doing anything different than any of you."

"It happens sometimes. Horses get their favorites, and there's not too much you can do about it. The good news is – with horses like that – if you're their person, they will turn themselves inside out for you, jump the moon, you name it."

"I know, but this isn't going to help him when it comes time to list him for sale. I doubt Ian will keep him as one of his personal mounts unless he gets his act together. Coop hasn't ridden him too much and is going to get on him later this week. I'm curious to see how that goes."

"I'm sure Coop can get him around alright – but Cap's mind is made up. You're it for him."

Erin wouldn't lie, it warmed her heart to know that she was Cap's person. Everyone wants to be someone's favorite, even if that someone is a horse. But his attachment to Erin would ultimately end up making his own life difficult. If Ian did decide to sell, hopefully Captain would take a liking to someone else the way he had with Erin. But you just never knew with horses.

After walking a couple laps around the ring to cool out Cap, Erin dismounted and lowered the jumps back to their original position. Then she shouted to Laney to have a nice ride and headed back to the barn, her one-woman horse in tow.

"You know I adore you," she said to Captain as she clipped him into cross-ties and began untacking. "But you need to be more flexible. You need to be able to be ridden by a lot of different people, and you need to behave while doing it. None of this launching Laney to the roof or going through your paces all stiff like a wooden horse for Ian." She grabbed a curry comb and started massaging Cap's back where the saddle had sat. "I only want the best for you, that's all. I'm leaving here next week, and I need to know that you're going to be a good boy after I'm gone."

"I'd like to talk to you about that actually," came Ian's voice behind her. Erin gave a little jump. "Sorry – didn't mean to sneak up on you…or interrupt your conversation," he smiled as he came over and gave Cap a nice pat on the neck.

Erin laughed. "You caught me – I just love talking to them."

"Do they talk back to you?"

"Of course they do!" she laughed.

"Horse people," Ian said with a slight shake of his head. "We're all alike, aren't we? Anyway, I wanted to talk about your contract. I know you're due to leave us next week, but I've really enjoyed working with you, and I love how the horses go for you. I'd like to offer you an extension – it can be month-by-month if you'd like – and it will be paid. All I ask is that when you're ready to leave, you give me two weeks' notice. What do you say?"

"I say yes! I would love to stay on for a bit."

"The pay's not much, but it's more than you're making now," he said with a laugh since Erin wasn't getting paid anything at the moment. "You'll still be considered a working student, just a paid one. As far as I'm concerned, stay as long as you'd like." He held out his hand and Erin quickly shook it.

"Thank you so much. I appreciate all the opportunities you've given me already, and I'm thrilled to stay on a bit longer."

"Great, glad to have you. There's an event at Morven Park that I'd like to take you to in mid-April. I want to put you on Panther and have you ride Intermediate. It's a step up for you, but you're ready, and

Pan will take care of you."

"Count me in! Thank you for trusting me with Panther."

"It's my pleasure, and Panther will love it. She's been semi-retired for the last year, so she'll be like a kid in a candy shop going out again." Ian paused to give Captain another rub on the neck. "How'd this one go today?"

"Perfect, as usual."

"Horses are so interesting, aren't they? I'm glad he's going well for you – I'd rather him go well for one person than be horrible across the board. But that's going to make his life tough down the road."

"That's what I was telling him as you walked over."

"Coop will ride him later this week, and then we'll go from there. I'm confident we can figure him out…and if not, well then looks like you got yourself another horse!" He said as he clapped Erin on the shoulder and walked away.

Another horse? Not sure I'm ready for that!

Chapter 27

As expected, Macy and Molly were excited to learn that Erin's contract had been extended and she'd been given more opportunities to learn from Ian. Also as expected, Erin's mom, Karen, was not excited.

"I was counting the days until you'd be home – only eight more to go, or so I thought," Karen sighed into the phone.

"Oh mom, stop being so dramatic," Erin laughed. "I'm not going to stay forever – maybe another month or two, tops. You don't want me to miss out on competing Panther, do you? That mare competed in the Olympics! Riding her is a once in a lifetime opportunity."

"I know, and of course I think it's fantastic you get to event Panther; I'm just being a selfish mother, that's all. I want my kids close to home."

"Well I promise you I'll be home soon – maybe by summer. In the meantime, mark your calendar – April 17th is the event at Morven Park. You've got to come watch."

"I wouldn't miss it. My daughter's Intermediate debut! My goodness I don't know if my heart will stand it."

"I know the jumps are higher, but Panther is a beast. We'll nail it. I can't wait!"

"I know you will sweetheart. But all the same, maybe I'll leave your father at home. I get scared watching you fly over those formidable obstacles, but at least I understand the sport and your talent. He would just die," Karen laughed. Rick, for all his years around horses, still didn't get his wife and daughters' obsession. But he knew horses made them happy, so that was enough for him.

"Yeah, as much as I'd love to see dad, maybe it's best he not come to watch this one. He can come to some of my lower level events closer to home."

"Oh, and that reminds me – I meant to tell you. I saw Leo's mom walking into the store the other day. I was already in the car and driving out so I couldn't stop to chat, but I was just curious – have you kept in touch with him at all?"

God love Karen. She just wanted the best for Erin and was petrified at the thought of her daughter being alone. What she didn't understand was that Erin was enjoying her freedom and solitude. True, Cooper was in the picture, and that was something Karen wasn't aware of, but it was casual. They would be parting at the end of May when he went home, and even though Erin knew a part of her heart would break when they separated, she knew she wasn't ready to commit to anyone, not even him.

"Not really. We've texted a few times, but that's about it. I've been so busy, and honestly, I just don't want to feel tied down right now. I don't want to feel obligated to have to call someone every day and check in or make time for a visit when my days are already filled to the brim as it is."

"I understand, my dear. I was just curious. Maybe you two can reconnect when you come home."

"You never know." And that was the truth. You never knew where life would take you. A year ago, all Erin could think about was her separation from Kevin and wonder if she'd made the right decision. She had gone from beating herself up over it to feeling relieved that she was moving on. And now she was at Emerald Isle Farm in Virginia preparing for her Intermediate debut with a horse who had won individual bronze at the

Olympics. What a ride the last year had been – lots of lows, but plenty of highs too.

"I heard Ian extended your contract, that's great news!" Chirped Laney the next day as the two began morning feedings. "I've really enjoyed working with you."

"Thanks! You all have been so helpful and welcoming, especially to a complete newbie like myself. Working here has been the best thing to happen to me in a long time."

"I'm glad to hear it. You deserve it after the year you've had." Erin and Laney had gotten to be pretty close, and Laney knew how difficult the last year of Erin's life had been.

Erin smiled at her friend as she continued to portion out the morning grain.

"Did you hear that Ian's taking us to Morven to do some serious cross country schooling tomorrow?" Laney asked as she grabbed the Farrier's Formula supplement to add to her feed mixtures.

"No, I hadn't! That will be such great practice."

"He mentioned it last night when we were doing night check. He wants you to take Panther so you can get a feel of her and the grounds before the event."

"Oh my goodness – I can't wait! Now that's all I'll be able to think about all day!"

Erin was up bright and early the following morning – so early, in fact, that she beat everyone else down. The quicker they got through their morning chores, the sooner they could load up the horses and head to Morven.

Her phone beeped as she was sorting through Panther's tack. It was a text from Macy.

M: Good luck today!
E: Thanks! I won't lie...kinda scared lol
M: Don't be! Put your big girl pants on and go for it!
E: I'm here for a good time, not for a long time, right?
M: That's the spirit! Besides, I thought you've competed Intermediate before?
E: No, only Preliminary. I schooled a handful of Intermediate jumps years ago in college, but that was ages ago.
M: Well you've got this. I believe in you.
E: Thanks love

Intermediate meant Erin would be taking jumps that were 3'9" and the cross country obstacles would be sturdier and more menacing. She'd have to ride forward and aggressive to make it around clean and in good time. But she knew Panther would be up to the challenge. That horse lived and breathed eventing and loved her job more than most.

Soon the barn came alive as everyone else arrived and began throwing grain and turning out horses. They hustled to get everything done in time so they could load up and hit the road at a decent hour. Ian wanted to get home in time to still work a few of the other horses that afternoon.

Erin had Panther's tack and gear packed in the trailer and ready to go. Ian would be riding another seasoned pro, Dilemma, and Cooper and Laney would be on their personal horses. Panther knew something was up when Erin entered her stall and gave her a last quick grooming. The mare was antsy as Erin placed the halter over her head and snapped the lead rope to the bottom; she admired the horse as she led her out into the aisle and outside to the waiting trailer. She was stunning – all black, not a speck of white anywhere, 17 hands, and eager to get going. This was going to be a fun day!

Morven Park was almost an hour's drive, and Ian went through the game plan with the others as he drove carefully along. They'd warm up in the outdoor jump ring, flat around and take a few cross-rails, then they'd head out cross country. The sun was shining, it was a cool sixty degrees, and Erin couldn't believe her good fortune. She was getting ready for an important cross country school with one of her long-time idols out in the bucolic Virginia countryside. This time a year ago she'd been stuck in her stuffy office in downtown Baltimore, dreaming about breaking free and forging a new path. And here she was.

Panther jigged quietly beside Erin as she led her down the trailer's ramp and walked her in a few circles. The mare was excited, but she was also a pro who knew how to behave. There wouldn't be any explosions or theatrics to worry about, but Erin would need to be on point today in order to keep up with her. She'd ridden her many times at home but had never taken her outside the ring, so this would be fantastic experience.

"Ready to jump all the things?" Laney asked Erin as they warmed their horses up in the outdoor.

"I've waited my whole life for this day."

"I'll take plenty of videos for you to study later. Jester and I will only be going over some of the Training jumps today, then we'll just tag along and watch you guys." Cooper would be taking Lucy over the Preliminary jumps, and after he coached his students through their training sessions, Ian would most likely take a few Advanced jumps with his horse, Dilemma.

And jump all the things they did! Erin couldn't remember having this much fun on a horse's back. Riding Panther was life-changing – there is something to be said for an upper level, been there/done that horse. There were multiple times when Erin made a mistake on the approach, but Panther fixed it – the horse knew when her rider was slightly off and made the adjustments herself.

They flew over huge roll tops and trakehners. They squeezed through skinnies and corners. They soared down banks and drop fences. Erin didn't blink as they sailed over ditches and down into sunken roads. The only one that gave her pause was the dreaded table jump. Erin considered herself a brave rider, but tables were her nemesis. Built similar to a wooden picnic table, they were solid, tall, and wide, meant to test the horse's scope. Erin could feel herself backing off as they galloped up to one when Cooper saw it and yelled, "Ride her forward! Leg! Now!" But Panther, having tackled too many tables to count in her career, didn't break stride and flew over in one huge leap despite Erin's hesitance.

"I think we've found your weakness," said Ian as Erin cantered back over to join the group. "I know they're intimidating – the spread is wider than anything you've ever jumped before. But you just gotta push yourself up and over it. You need the strongest possible approach. Panther knows what to do, but any other horse will feel your hesitancy and back off – and that's when you get hurt. Do it again."

Erin swallowed her fear and took the table three more times. By the last jump, she was feeling somewhat comfortable – enough that, she hoped, she wouldn't give it a second thought when she came to it on course during her competition.

As they made their way back to the trailer, happy with their session but completely spent, Erin thanked Ian for his generosity in letting her ride and compete his beloved mare.

"She certainly took care of me today," she said as she gave the mare's neck a sweet pat. "I can't thank you enough for sharing her with me."

"You're very welcome. Keep this up and I think you two are going to turn some heads on the big day."

Chapter 28

Later that afternoon, Erin was back at the farm and finishing her last ride of the day. After another wonderful work-out, she was cooling out Captain with an easy walk on the buckle. She was still elated from her cross country session earlier and couldn't think about anything other than the upcoming event.

Cap, head down and stretching through his neck and back, plodded around slowly while Erin watched Cooper turn out the horse he'd just been working. He saw her and waved from a distance, then began to make his way over to her.

"You looked great today," he said with an easy smile. "I think my little lassie is going to be a force to be reckoned with in the future."

"I certainly hope so." It was so nice to hear such positive feedback from a rider as talented and experienced as Cooper. It validated all of her hard work…and the tough decisions she'd had to make to get to this point.

"I think after the Morven horse trials everyone's going to remember the name Erin Sorrenson."

"Okay now you're just flattering me," she laughed softly.

"No, I'm serious. This is one of the first larger events of the season. I think you'll be surprised at the number of big dogs that will be there."

"I wish you hadn't said that – now I'll be even more nervous."

"No need to be – Panther is an upper level unicorn. She'll take care of you then like she did today. Although I must say, you definitely held your own."

"I tried. I'm sure there were plenty of times when she was like, what are you doing up there woman?!"

Coop laughed. "Don't you wish we could read our horses' minds?"

"Sometimes. Other times it's probably best we're left in the dark! I'm sure Panther was uttering some expletives at me today – especially when we were jumping the table."

"The table used to get me as well – drop fences too. We all have that one that we struggle with; the trick is to just keep at it. Soon you won't even remember that it used to bother you."

"Here's hoping." Erin dismounted and rolled up her stirrups. Cooper came over and with Captain essentially standing between them and the barn, blocking anyone from seeing, Cooper pulled Erin into a sweet kiss.

"I miss you," he whispered in her ear. They'd had a couple early mornings, so Erin hadn't made her nightly visit for a few days.

"I miss you too. I'll be over tonight."

"I don't know how I'm going to bring myself to pack up and leave you. I've been looking forward to going home for months…and now I'm dreading it."

"So then stay."

"Is that really what you want?"

Erin thought for a moment…and in her heart, she just wasn't sure. This had been such a tumultuous year with one huge change after another. She knew she couldn't fully commit to Cooper – not in the way she should if she was going to ask him to stay. It wouldn't be fair to him to uproot his life and his plans for her. Not when she was still so unsure of herself.

"Honestly…I'm don't know," she replied sadly. Erin wished she had all the answers, and she wondered if she would live to regret letting this man go, but she didn't have a choice.

Cooper placed his finger under her chin and lifted it until they made eye contact. "It's okay, lass. It's okay." And they kissed again.

Deep down, Erin knew that she was falling in love with Cooper, but she also felt that she couldn't trust herself. She'd been through so much, and she knew she still had a ways to go before she was completely whole again, healed from the divorce and the changes life had thrown her way. Erin was confident that she was on the right path, but until she felt settled, she couldn't drag Cooper into her mess.

"Happy birthday to you! Happy birthday to you! Happy birthday dear Laney – happy birthday to you!" The Emerald Isle team sang as the waiter placed a large slice of cake in front of the birthday girl. After the song ended, Laney blew out the candle and made the customary wish.

"Thank you so much – I really appreciate you all coming out to celebrate," she smiled sincerely at the group.

Earlier in the day Ian had declared that they should all finish up no later than five o'clock that night so they could clean up and head into the town of Middleburg for Laney's birthday dinner. Laney chose her favorite restaurant in the area – The Red Fox Inn & Tavern – and Erin couldn't wait to try it. Adam had taken Macy there the previous year when in town for Valentine's Day, and Macy had raved about the food and atmosphere.

Sitting in the main dining room with her back to the fireplace, Erin was in heaven. The day had been cool – it was early April after all – so the fire's warmth had been a welcome respite after a day spent out of doors.

From the appetizers to the cocktails, from the main entrée of shrimp and grits to the flourless chocolate cake for dessert, Erin's entire meal was delicious. She made a mental note to text Macy later that evening to tell her of her experience.

"Here is a little something from me and Cooper," Erin said as she handed Laney a brightly-colored wrapped package. Ian had recently reminded the group that Laney's birthday was coming up, so Erin had zipped down to Horse Country again to pick up something for her. Of course, the owner, Marion, was on hand and helped Erin pick out the perfect present for her friend.

"You didn't have to get me anything," Laney cried in delight as she began unwrapping the gift.

"I know, but we wanted to. You've been such an incredible help to me on my new journey here that it's the least I could do."

"Oh my goodness – they're perfect!" She held up a new pair of spurs. "How did you know I needed new ones?"

"I saw you putting yours on when we were schooling at Morven the other day. The leather on the right one looked like it was about to snap it was so worn," Erin told her.

"Thank you so much!" Laney got up and hugged Erin and Cooper. "You two are so sweet. And thank you for dinner," she said as she hugged Ian as well.

"Nothing's too good for my favorite assistant trainer," he said with a wink. With Cooper's upcoming departure, Ian had promoted Laney to assistant trainer.

"Hey – I thought I was your favorite," laughed Coop as that was still his title as well.

"Sorry, Laney works harder than you do," he said as he playfully clapped Coop on the back. "You're my favorite cousin though, so there you go."

"Gee, thanks Ian," Cooper replied sadly. He was just playing along though and was quick to laugh after.

The table then ordered a round of coffees and continued their conversations about, what else, horses. The Morven event was just over a week away, and Erin had taken Panther out multiple times at the farm so she could get a really good feel for the horse. Big things were heading her way very soon – she could just feel it.

Chapter 29

Dressage had gone well, really well, actually. Erin's test had been complicated, like all Intermediate tests should be, but Panther knew her job and Erin had been able to ignore the butterflies fluttering around in her stomach long enough to put in a stellar performance.

In another hour they'd complete their stadium jumping round and then head out directly to tackle cross country.

Laney and Cooper were competing as well and were busy with their own horses, so Erin was thankful her mom and Macy had made the long drive down to support her and help when needed. Molly was supposed to come but had woken up feeling ill that morning.

"She thinks it's food poisoning," Karen said as she held Panther while Erin removed her dressage saddle. "Apparently they ate at some new restaurant last night, and she's been sick to her stomach all morning."

"Poor thing," Erin said sympathetically. She knew firsthand that food poisoning was no fun, but she had also been looking forward to seeing her sister. "I hope it doesn't last too long."

"Should be out of her system within twenty-four hours, fingers crossed." Even though they were full grown, Karen hated it when either of her daughters were sick. "I started some chicken soup in the crock pot before I left. If it's done before I'm home, I'll have your father run it over to her."

Erin smiled. She knew she'd been extremely blessed with two very caring and loving parents. They didn't always see eye-to-eye on everything, but that was okay. Everyone had each other's back, and that's what mattered.

"I'll give her a call as soon as I'm finished and see how she's doing," Erin said as she gave Panther another thorough brushing. She wanted to be sure that the mare shined.

"I can't get over this horse," said Macy adoringly as she ran a hand down Panther's neck and over her back. "She's just stunning, and so well put together."

"She's a star, that's for sure. When Ian got her, she was as green as could be. He brought her up completely himself. How satisfying to bring up a horse from baby green to the Olympics." And Erin still couldn't believe she was the one riding her today.

Ian had walked up with Erin before her dressage test, giving her some last minutes tips and advice. Now he was off with Cooper who was riding in his Prelim test at that very moment. Coaching three different riders in three separate divisions meant a lot of running back and forth between rings, the trailer, and the cross country course. But Ian loved every moment of it.

A few minutes later Laney appeared leading Jester. They had been warming up in one of the schooling rings preparing for their dressage test later that morning. "I stopped by the office – they already had your division's dressage scores up. Want to know where you stand?" She asked with a teasing smile.

Sometimes competitors didn't want to know the standings before continuing on with the competition because it added pressure, especially if you were in the top three or four. Having that knowledge going into the next phases and wanting desperately to remain on top could sometimes just shake nerves even further.

"Tell me." Erin was not one of those competitors. She wanted all the facts.

"You're in first!"

"Well done!" Macy squealed as she high-fived Erin.

"I knew it," smiled Karen. "That test was just too darn good!" She hugged her daughter and then gave Panther a little rub on her forehead.

"I can't believe it," Erin was in shock. "I knew it was good, but I wasn't sure it was first place good. Now I just need to keep it!"

And she did. Their stadium jumping round was strong and clean. Erin knew that not only would she need to be clean without any jump faults, but she'd have to be fast without any time penalties. Before entering the ring, Ian reminded her that Panther was incredibly light on her feet and could cut tight corners if necessary to shave off a few seconds here and there.

"Check your watch – if you see you're running a little slow, get moving. Cut some corners if you have time. This is Panther you're riding – she knows the drill. With Jazzy and Captain, you still have the mindset to make it a good experience and not rush them along. Panther's different – she knows her job and gets after it."

They zoomed around the course, clearing jump after jump with never so much as a rub on a rail.

"I'm never giving her back," Erin joked to Ian as they exited the ring.

"She certainly is having a great time with you up there. You guys look like you've been doing this forever."

Erin could not think of a better compliment. She was beaming as they made their way over to the start of cross country. With about twenty minutes until her time, she walked Panther to keep her limber. When she was on deck, her loved ones wished her best of luck and Ian reminded her to attack the jumps – especially that table.

"Keep a strong pace the entire time. Check your watch – you remember where you need to be on course at certain times, right?"

"Yes."

"Good. Once she gets into her rhythm, let her keep it. Try and stay out of her way on the approaches as best you can. She can see the distances too, don't forget that."

"I won't." At this point, nerves were kicking in.

"Good luck. You've got this. Coop said to tell you good luck as well." Cooper was busy with Lucy, so he couldn't be there to see Erin off.

As soon as they took off, Erin's nerves disappeared in an instant and it was all red on right for the rest of the way.

The table jump came and went without Erin so much as batting an eye, and she was amazed at the horse beneath her. Panther was doing what she loved most in this world; she got into her rhythm just like Ian said she would, and Erin stayed with her every step of the way.

This is my life now. This is what I want to be doing.

As they took the last jump and then galloped for home, Erin had tears in her eyes. She'd finished her first Intermediate event with no faults or time penalties. She and Panther had won decisively!

Later that afternoon during the ribbon ceremony, Erin was all smiles as they pinned the blue ribbon to Panther's bridle. She also happily accepted a large silver award tray which was engraved with the event's title and date, and after smiling for what seemed like a million pictures, Erin led out the victory gallop. No victory had ever felt sweeter.

Chapter 30

As is always the case after a long horse show day, Erin was exhausted by early evening. They arrived home dirty, tired, yet happy as it had been a great day for the farm with Cooper taking sixth in Preliminary and Laney taking third in Training. And, of course, Erin's big win in Intermediate was the icing on the cake.

Pulling into the farm meant the day was almost over, but there were still horses to unload and care for, tack and gear to clean and put away, and even more horses to feed and turn out.

"Thank you for today," Erin said softly as she stroked Panther's neck while the mare dug into her evening grain. "You have no idea how grateful I am to you." Horses that taught you and took you to the next level were worth their weight in gold. Erin would forever feel indebted to the mare who willingly carried her through her first Intermediate course – and of course she'd never be able to thank Ian enough for giving her all of these opportunities.

With all of her chores done, it was time to head up to her apartment, make something to eat, and fall fast asleep in her bed. But Cooper had other ideas.

C: Want to come over for a celebratory dinner? I'm cooking!
E: I'm exhausted but could be tempted. What's on the menu?
C: Nothing fancy – some fried chicken. It's my special recipe though.
E: Well I don't want to miss out on that.
C: It would be the biggest regret of your life.
E: Lol. Okay – hopping in the shower now and then I'll be there.

Even though time had sprung forward, it was still dark by the time Erin towel dried her hair, threw on a sweatshirt, and snuck out of the barn to Cooper's house. When he opened the door, she was hit with the most delicious smells coming from the kitchen, and she realized then just how hungry she actually was.

"Smells amazing. Thanks for having me over."

"I figured you'd be too tired to make yourself something decent, and a champ shouldn't go to bed on an empty stomach," Cooper said as he leaned in to give Erin a quick kiss.

"You're right. My plan was to make some eggs, but even that seemed like too much effort. It was probably just going to be cereal."

"Well then this will seem like a feast." He turned to head back into the kitchen to put the finishing touches on the chicken, mashed potatoes, and green beans. It was simple, yet perfect comfort food after a long, tiring day.

Erin grabbed some plates, silverware, and napkins and set the little table on the far wall of the kitchen. She then filled two glasses with water and grabbed a beer for Cooper from the fridge. She thought about having one herself, but when she was really tired like she was now, any alcohol would put her right to sleep. And she wanted to stay awake long enough to enjoy a meal with her favorite guy.

"Sit down and relax," Coop motioned to a chair at the table. "This is almost done."

"I could get used to this," she smiled sweetly. When she and Kevin had been married, they had eaten most of their dinners out. It had been so easy to do in the city where everything was within walking distance. When they stayed in, they had cooked together, and even though the food had been edible, neither were gifted in the kitchen. Cooper definitely looked like he knew what he was doing, and Erin couldn't wait to dive into the meal, especially the mashed potatoes.

"So, how do you feel? You competed in and won your first Intermediate event," Cooper asked as he brought over the chicken and sat the plate on a potholder.

"It doesn't seem real yet. I keep looking at the blue ribbon and can't believe I actually won it."

"Bet it felt good to win with your mom and Macy there too."

"Oh yeah, they're my biggest fans. Molly too. I'm sorry she couldn't make it."

"I'm one of your biggest fans too, you know," he winked as he brought the rest of the food over and sat down.

"Are you now?" She asked coyly.

"I am. And I'm looking forward to watching you go far in this sport. You'll be competing in your first Advanced before you know it."

Erin exhaled a deep breath. "I don't know about that. One step at a time."

"You'll get there." He grabbed Erin's plate and served her a hearty portion of everything.

"This is delicious," Erin complimented him as she began shoveling chicken into her mouth. "What's so secret about your secret recipe?"

"I can't tell you."

"Are you going to have to kill me?"

"Kill you…or marry you. It's a family secret, so I can't tell you unless you're family." His eyes were serious, but Erin knew he was joking.

"Well I guess we'll just have to keep the mystery going. I'm sure you'll tell me one day."

"At our wedding."

"Or my funeral," Erin said with a wicked smile.

"Definitely one or the other."

Dinner was wonderful and just what Erin needed to refuel after a long yet exhilarating day. She marveled at how easily she and Cooper chatted with one another, how much they had in common, and the ease with which they could joke around. Erin felt like she'd known Cooper for years, not just a few months. She realized with a pang that he'd leave a large gaping hole in her life and her heart when he left for Ireland.

But she wouldn't think about that now. She was an Intermediate level eventer. Today was only for happy thoughts.

After dinner Cooper grabbed another beer, and they sat on the couch together watching videos of their runs from the day. Erin still couldn't believe it when she saw herself riding Panther, launching over the most daunting jumps she'd ever taken. And she looked so confident.

"You guys look fierce," Cooper said as they watched her take the table jump.

"I was just thinking how confident I looked."

"But did you feel confident?"

Erin thought for a moment. "Yeah, I did. I remember thinking, okay three more jumps until the table, two more, one more…and then when it came, we flew over before it could even register that it had come. Does that make sense?"

"Absolutely. When you're in the moment like that, you do what has to be done. Right then and there, you just do it. And then you think about it later."

"That's exactly what it was like."

"I'm proud of you."

Erin looked up at Cooper and kissed him softly. "Thanks. You don't know how much your support means to me."

She laid her head against his chest while they

swiped through a few more pictures and videos…and then Erin fell fast asleep.

Cooper was snoring softly when Erin woke up about two hours later. It was just after midnight. She pulled a light blanket up to his chin, gave him a soft kiss on his cheek, and let herself out the door.

The walk back to the barn was cool and refreshing. The little catnap she took had given her a second wind, and by the time she reached the barn, she was wide awake.

And so was Laney. Erin had rounded the corner and bumped right into her.

"Sorry!" Erin squealed as she grabbed Laney to keep her from stumbling. "I had no idea you'd be up!"

Laney grinned wickedly at her friend. "But I knew you'd be," she said with a sly wink.

"What does that mean?" Erin had been caught so off guard she couldn't think on her feet.

"I couldn't sleep, so I came down to check on everyone…and well…I know about you and Cooper. I've known for quite some time now."

"Well, shit."

Chapter 31

Laney invited Erin back to her apartment where she made them some chamomile tea, and then they both curled up on the couch. Laney's apartment was the mirror image of Erin's, except that it looked more lived in, which would make sense since Laney had been there over a year at this point. Unlike Erin's room, objects covered every surface – books, ribbons, gear, framed photos – but it wasn't messy or cluttered. It just looked like someone was planning to stay for a while.

"So how long have you known?" Erin asked as she blew on her tea to cool it.

"At least a month."

"How did you figure it out?" Cooper was going to be just as shocked as Erin – they both thought they were being so sneaky.

"Well, for one, I have eyes. I see the way you two look at each other. The little glances, the winks and knowing smiles. And two, these walls are paper thin, so I'd hear you leave just after dark and then come back a few hours later. I suffer with borderline insomnia, so more often than not, I'm awake."

"And here we thought we were being so discreet."

"Once I was out in the barn – I sometimes just go down and check on everyone when I really can't get to sleep – but I never turn on the lights. I was peeking into Captain's stall when I saw you walk back in."

"I'm such an idiot."

"No, you aren't. We don't care what you guys do."

"We? Please tell me Ian doesn't know."

Laney laughed a little at Erin's panic-stricken

face. "He does, but he only figured it out recently too. I didn't tell him."

"What did he say?!"

"He figured it out like I did – saw the way you guys looked at each other. It was only last week though that he put it together. I was tacking up Jester when he walked over and asked if I knew about you two. I told him that I'd suspected but neither of you had said anything. He said, 'Well it sounds like they want to keep it quiet, so don't say anything to them.'"

Erin dropped her head into her hands. "Well isn't this great?"

Laney reached over and patted Erin's leg. "Hey, don't sweat it. Ian doesn't care – and you know I don't. I think you guys make a cute couple. Besides, this is very common. I've never been at a barn where people *weren't* hooking up."

"I just want to remain completely professional – especially in Ian's eyes. I'm new to the industry and this is my first working student position. I don't want to be known as the girl who hops into everyone's bed."

"You aren't. And you've been incredibly professional since day one. Don't beat yourself up – everyone does it."

"Have you?"

"Of course. At my last job I was in a pretty serious relationship with the assistant trainer."

"What happened?"

"He was given the opportunity to start his own barn with another friend. They were going in together – but the barn was in Florida. And we were here in Virginia."

"Why didn't you go with him?"

"Because he didn't really ask me to. It was kind of a half-hearted invitation, but I didn't want to move to

Florida anyway. We both knew the relationship had run its course."

"He didn't consider staying here with you?"

Laney laughed. "Not for a second. But in his defense, had I been offered a similar deal, I would have taken it too. Significant other be damned."

"Wow – this is a ruthless game."

"We all have the same goal – get to the top and stay there. I didn't get into this industry for the guys. I did it for the horses."

"I understand."

"So, are you two serious? Is Coop still planning on going back to Ireland?"

"He is. And I'm planning on going home to Maryland too – probably around the same time, but I haven't decided yet. Neither of us want to be the one to ask the other to stay. I, for one, am just not ready for a serious relationship. I haven't even been officially divorced for a year yet. I'm not in any position to ask someone to give up their hopes and plans and follow me back home."

"What if he wants to? What if it's not as big of a sacrifice as you think it is?"

"He's been talking about going home since I got here. It's one of the very first things he mentioned. It's his home – and I get that. And I still need to figure out some things on my end. You know – like what I'm going to do with the rest of my life once I leave here."

"Do you have any ideas?"

"I do...I just haven't really told anyone yet. I mentioned it briefly to Macy once, but I'm still kind of rolling things around in my mind."

"Well I'm all ears if you want to talk about it."

"I appreciate that. You've been a good friend to me here – that's meant a lot."

"My approach is that you can never have enough friends in this industry. Some people think the exact opposite – that everyone is the enemy, the competition. And while, yes, other riders and trainers are your competition, we all need to be able to lean on one another occasionally."

"That's very smart – good words of wisdom for sure." Erin sighed. "So do you think I should address my dalliance with Ian?"

"I wouldn't. Believe me when I say that he doesn't care. I think he thought it was funny, the way you guys were working so hard to hide it."

"Well I want him – and you – to know that it hasn't and won't get in the way of my work."

"We know that. Trust me, you're putting way too much thought into this. Ian knows you're hardworking and great at what you do. What you do during your time off isn't anyone's concern."

A sense of relief washed over Erin as she made her way back to her apartment a few minutes later. Laney had put her mind at ease, and while Erin wasn't going to advertise her relationship with Cooper, she didn't feel the need to sneak around in the middle of the night anymore. Maybe she'd even spend the entire night there – at least she'd get some decent sleep instead of forcing herself to walk back to her room in the early morning hours.

Chapter 32

The following morning Erin was making herself a cup of coffee when Cooper walked through the tack room and, making sure no one else was around, leaned in for a quick kiss.

"Morning lass," he whispered in her ear.

"The jig is up," Erin said as she stirred a bit more creamer into her cup.

"What jig?"

"Our jig. I ran into Laney last night on my way back from your place. She knows about us – Ian does too."

"Get out. We've been so quiet – and you're like a stealthy little ninja making your way back and forth every night."

"Well apparently Laney is an insomniac, so she heard me coming and going."

"And Ian?"

Erin smiled. "He told Laney he could tell because of the way we look at each other."

Cooper slowly pulled Erin to him. "Well now, I can't help that. Guess the eyes don't lie – windows to the soul, as they say." He leaned down and gave Erin a soft, sensual kiss. Now that their secret was out, who cared if anyone saw.

Their kiss was interrupted by Erin's phone. "I have to take this," she said as she, reluctantly, extracted herself out of Cooper's embrace. "But we can pick this up again later – you know – in broad daylight this time."

She answered the phone as she headed for the door of the tack room. "Hey Adam! Thanks for returning my call." That was all Coop could hear before Erin exited the room and rounded the corner of the barn aisle, out of sight.

The morning and early afternoon went by in a blur with the general hustle and bustle common in a large training barn. Erin had fallen into a blissful routine with riding, horse care, and occasional chit chat with her colleagues who had turned into friends.

She had her weekly lesson with Jazzy, and Erin was pleased by the mare's continued progress.

"We might have another Panther on our hands," Ian said as he walked back to the barn with Erin after her lesson. She had schooled in the outdoor ring, and Erin was over-the-moon at the compliment.

"You think so?" She knew Jazzy was talented but hearing it from Ian confirmed it.

"Absolutely. She has incredible scope, work ethic, you name it. She reminds me so much of Panther when she was that age. Keep her healthy and sound and you guys have a bright future ahead of you."

Erin hummed happily to herself as she untacked her horse and led her to the wash stall. The temperatures were on their way up, so a quick hosing down after workouts had become necessary.

"Someone's in a good mood," Cooper said as he passed by on his way to the ring, Lucy in tow.

"Ian just compared Jazzy to Panther. I can't believe it," she grinned from ear to ear.

"I can. You guys are already quite the team."

"You free tonight?"

"You know it."

"Let's go out to dinner – my treat. I have some news I want to share with you."

"Sounds like good news to me. It's a date. A very public date," he laughed as he led his mare off for their training session.

    As is the case with horses and animal care, evening chores ran a little long, so Erin and Cooper decided to just zip down the road for dinner at The Front Porch. The little restaurant was packed, but they found a table for two in a quiet corner.

    Erin couldn't help admiring Cooper in his simple polo green shirt that offset his red hair. As the weather warmed and he spent more time outside, the sun had lightened his hair to a beautiful strawberry blond. His green eyes glowed; his face was tan despite his Irish roots. Erin couldn't believe she was going to let this man go.

    After placing their orders and handing the menus back to the waiter, Cooper reached forward and took Erin's hands in his.

    "So, tell me your big news."

    Erin took a deep breath. This was something she'd been thinking about for quite some time, but she'd never really thought she could put her plan into action. But she was making it happen, and interestingly, Adam, Macy's boyfriend, had been the first to officially know, but that was because he had a large part to play in it.

    "When I leave here – and I'm not completely sure when that will be – I'm going to start my own business. I'm not going back to law, not in any capacity. I'm going to start Sorrenson Sporthorses. I'll take Thoroughbreds who are retiring off the track, retrain them for second careers, and sell them. It's not a business that will make me a fortune in any way, but it will be one that I love. One that I'm passionate about. One that I'll look forward to getting out of bed every morning for.

    "I've already been in touch with Adam Cleary –

he's Macy's boyfriend – who also happens to be a racehorse trainer. He always has plenty of good quality, sound horses coming off the track looking for new jobs. I spoke with him earlier and he's agreed to send me as many as I can handle. Most of them will be like Jazzy – completely free – just in need of some education for another discipline. I love Thoroughbreds and the idea of helping prepare them for a new life."

She paused for breath and looked at Cooper – his face was serious, but she thought she detected a smile in his eyes. "What do you think?"

He cleared his throat and squeezed her hands. "I think it's perfect."

"You do?"

"I do. You have the talent to bring these horses along and set them up on a new path for success. It also gives you the time to keep bringing Jazzy along, compete her, and maybe compete the new ones too. Give them as much experience as possible before reselling them."

"You're the first person I've really told – well, beside Adam, but that's because I think I can get most of the horses I need through him. You don't think I'm crazy, do you? I think my parents will flip."

"I don't think you're crazy. You've got to follow your heart. So many people hate their jobs; they wake up every day, miserable. People like us, in the horse industry, we won't die rich, but we'll die happy. We get up every morning excited to go to work, and that says more than anything else."

Erin breathed a sigh of relief. Having Cooper's support meant the world. He was intelligent and realistic, and if he thought she could do it, then that was all the encouragement she needed.

Shortly thereafter their meals arrived, and Erin chatted nonstop about her plans and ideas for the future.

Cooper asked a variety of questions, which forced Erin to think about all aspects of the business – not just the horses and the training. There was so much to consider, but for the first time in years, Erin felt giddy for what was to come. She had a lightness inside that told her she was getting closer to finding herself again. All the self-doubt about her marriage and having children – all the worry that she was making irreversible mistakes – it was vanishing. And in its place was a newfound confidence she hadn't felt in ages.

Later that night, Cooper took her back to his place and as they made love, Erin's heart broke knowing that their time was coming to an end. While discussing the future of Erin's business, they had deliberately not mentioned *their* future.

As Cooper caressed her cheek and kissed her softly, she noticed a sadness in his eyes that she was sure mirrored in her own. Sure, she could ask him not to go back to Ireland, to come home with her to Maryland. But then what? Erin had just figured out what she was going to do with her professional life – she wasn't ready to tackle her personal life. She would be soon, but not just yet. And until she was ready, it wasn't fair to ask Cooper to sacrifice his dreams of going home and helping run his family's business. They were counting on him too, and Erin wouldn't be selfish.

Chapter 33

Erin blinked and it was early May. It was finally here – the month in which Cooper would pack up his belongings, say goodbye to the team, and head home. They had just one last month together.

The thought of saying farewell to a man she had come to care deeply for dampened her spirits, but the weather tried its best to lift them. The temperatures were warm, the flowers were in bloom, and the earth was a deep shade of green.

And the show schedule was filling up. Earlier in the day, the team had gathered in the tack room to go over calendars, pick events to attend, and figure out a plan of action for each horse. Of course, Cooper would be leaving at the end of the month and taking Lucy with him, but he would be all-in until that moment.

Erin wasn't sure when she'd be leaving, but to play it safe, she only entered events in the month of May. She'd be showing Jazzy, of course, as well as a few other greenies in training, like Captain.

Captain had continued with his not-so-secret love affair with Erin. Laney, Cooper, and Ian had all taken turns on him, and while none of them had been bucked off since Laney's earlier incident, it was clear that Captain only tried his hardest for Erin. The horse was a mystery, and only Erin had been able to solve him.

Erin had a few hours off in the mid-afternoon before evening feedings began, so she took advantage of the free time to hit the grocery store. On her way there, Molly called. She picked up and waited for the call to connect to her Bluetooth.

Erin had recently told Molly and Macy about her

plans to return home at some point and start her sporthorse business. As expected, both girls had been absolutely thrilled and thought it was the perfect solution for her new post-lawyer, post-divorce life. Erin still had to tell her parents about her new venture, but she was going to wait until she'd made up her mind about when to return home.

"Have you decided what you're going to do?" Molly asked. She knew her sister was conflicted on when she should move back home. Erin was comfortable at Ian's and even though she had a plan for when she did return, it was still scary to put all these new changes into motion.

"Not yet. I keep going back and forth. There are so many reasons to stay but just as many reasons to come home."

"Can I give you my two cents?"

"Of course." Erin valued her sister's thoughts.

"Do whatever you'd like, of course, it's your life. But – I'd love if you could come home and help me with Gypsy's training."

"Moll, you don't need me. You two have been doing wonderful and you know it."

"Well, let me rephrase. I would love if you could come home and train Gypsy for me...for the next six and a half months while I can't ride." Molly giggled.

Erin paused, letting everything sink in. "Holy shit! You're pregnant?"

Molly continued to laugh. "Yes! I'm almost three months. I found out a few weeks ago, but Beau and I didn't want to tell anyone until I was a bit further along. And since I can't ride until after the baby's here, well, I need you."

"I can't believe I'm going to be an aunt!"

"And you'll be the best Aunt Erin ever." Molly

paused for a moment. "I know children are a touchy subject for you right now, so I don't want to make you uncomfortable in any way…"

"Molly stop," Erin quickly cut her sister off. "Just because I didn't want to be a mother doesn't mean I don't want to be an aunt. You're my sister, and I love you to death. I can't wait for you to be a mom. Please don't ever worry about me, or what I'm thinking…trust me, I'm so happy for you and for our family!"

"So…does this mean you're coming home?" Molly asked hopefully.

"Yeah…I think it does. Cooper's leaving at the end of the month anyway and with you pregnant, I think it's time. I want to be close to help you with anything you need." All signs were pointing towards her going home and getting on with life.

"I can't wait to have you back."

Later that night when she climbed in Cooper's bed, she broke the news to him. She recounted Molly's call and told him that the timing just felt right.

"Even though I don't want to be a mom, I'm so excited to be an aunt. We've always had a pretty small family, so it will be nice to watch it grow. And…I also don't really want to be here without you anyway."

"Oh lass," Cooper said as he held her chin, lips brushing her forehead. "You know I'd go anywhere with you. You just have to ask." He'd been debating on telling her that for some time but hadn't wanted to appear pushy. He knew she'd been through a lot and didn't need to make any more life-changing decisions. But he also knew he'd regret not telling her how he felt.

"I know. And believe me, I want to ask you to come home with me – more than anything. But it wouldn't be fair."

"Why not?"

"Because I'm not 100% in here or here," she pointed to both her head and her heart. "I'm close. I'm figuring out my life a little bit more every day, but until I'm back, until I feel like me again, I can't ask you to give up Ireland for me. Also, if you want children one day, I can't give you that."

"Lass, I've told you. I don't care for children either...and I'm telling you, you *can* ask me to stay here. I want to be with you. I love you."

Erin's eyes started to glisten with unshed tears. "I know. I'm falling for you too. But I'm not the same person I was a year ago. I need to learn how to live the new life I'm creating for myself." She blinked and the tears cascaded down her cheeks. Was she making the biggest mistake of her life?

"I know you've had a lot of changes – and most of them unwanted. But I can help you pick up the pieces. I can help you build this new life. Let me. We'll build it together."

"I can't ask that of you. What if you end up hating the person I turn into?" He knew that she was thinking about her ex-husband and how he had turned on her when she realized she wasn't meant to be a mother. It had been a big decision, and a brave one at that, to acknowledge her desire to remain childless in a society that pushed kids, that made those who didn't want them feel like something was wrong, like they were outsiders. Erin had bucked the norm and had been shunned by her husband, the one person who should have had her back and supported her choice.

And now she was afraid of disappointing someone else. Cooper realized that it was easier for her to let him go. It was the safer decision because then she couldn't possibly disappoint him down the road. His heart ached for her, for how her past had scarred her.

"I could never hate you." He knew in his heart that this was true, but this would just sound like an empty promise to Erin. Years ago, her ex would have said the same thing. Cooper would just have to prove to Erin that she could trust him. That he wouldn't go back on his word – that he would only ever love her.

"I want to believe that. I really do."

"I'll prove it to you, lass. If it's the last thing I do."

Chapter 34

"So I hear you're leaving us," Laney said to Erin as she walked up behind her in the barn aisle.

Erin had given her notice to Ian earlier in the day, and word had gotten around quickly. Paul had already come up to her to tell her how much he would miss her.

"I am," she said sadly as she hugged her friend.

Laney embraced her tightly. "I'm going to miss you. Not sure what I'll do around here with both you and Coop gone."

Erin felt bad that she was leaving at the same time as Cooper, worried that she was leaving Laney and Ian in the lurch, but Ian assured her that he could find a replacement working student in no time. Erin had given him three weeks' notice, and Ian had a couple people in mind who would be right for the job.

"Well I'm here for a few more weeks, so put me to work!"

And work she did. Knowing that her time with the Emerald Isle team was coming to an end, Erin threw herself into her duties with renewed vigor. She wanted to leave on a wonderful note with very positive lasting impressions for everyone she worked with. And, of course, she wanted to make the most of her time under Ian's tutelage, so she rode around the clock, especially if Ian was nearby and could offer some guidance.

The team took a trailerful of horses to another nearby event and came home exhausted but clutching multiple ribbons. Erin and Jazzy had gotten a first in Beginner Novice, which she was thrilled about as it was Jazzy's first ever full event.

This particular event also had a CT portion where she showed Captain in just dressage and stadium jumping, and they, too, came home with a blue. It had been another great day for the farm, and Erin got a little misty-eyed on the drive back knowing that her days with this team were numbered.

Emailing Ian about a working student position had been a completely spur-of-the-moment idea, but it had truly turned into a defining moment. Quite simply, it had changed the trajectory of Erin's life. Gone was law and corporate America. Gone was working for a boss who expected her to put in eighty hours a week working with clients who were at some of the lowest points in their lives.

Now, every day, it was horses. Not every day was roses, of course. There was the proverbial blood, sweet, and tears. Horses acted up, tried to buck you off, injured themselves or colicked – you name it. But if you loved the animal the way Erin did, the way this team did, then there would always be more good days than bad.

As her time in Virginia drew to a close, Erin began to pack up her apartment and coordinate Jazzy's return as well. Molly and Karen would drive down with the horse trailer on Erin's last day and bring everyone home. Erin, who had driven down separately, would load up her SUV and drive behind the trailer.

She had finally told her parents about her plans for Sorrenson Sporthorses, and, to her surprise, both had been supportive. While they worried that her income would always be spotty as it depended upon the sale of horses – something you could never guarantee – they just wanted their daughter to be happy. And Erin also suspected that they truly didn't care what she was doing as long as she was home. She had only been about two hours away in Virginia, but her family was close-knit, and Erin knew her parents just wanted her back home where she belonged.

Her plan, for the short-term, was to move back in with Macy. Erin would stay there until she sorted some things out, and then she'd move into the carriage house that Molly had rented years ago. Erin had made some calls and learned that it would be vacant in two months, and she felt it was time to get out of Macy's hair. Not that Macy wanted her to leave – Erin knew she was welcome there – but Macy's relationship with Adam was progressing and the two were talking about moving in together. Adam would move into Macy's house and rent his out to his long-time assistant, Gil. Macy had insisted that Erin stay, regardless of Adam, but she didn't want it to be like three's company. It was time for her to find her own wings and fly.

For the time being, Erin would base the majority of her operation out of her parents' farm. Not only was the barn large enough to accommodate a number of horses, but Karen and Rick had built a gorgeous sand ring for the girls when they were younger. Even though Erin intended to get her trainees out into the fields and on the trails, she figured the ring would come in handy, especially in the beginning of each horse's retraining.

Macy also offered her farm for any overflow Erin might have and encouraged her friend to continue to treat the farm like her own. Erin didn't know if she could ever repay Macy for all that she'd done, from opening up her home when she and Kevin separated, to now opening up her farm to help Erin grow her business. It certainly takes a village, and Erin was grateful that her tribe was one in a million.

Two days before she was set to go home, Erin looked around her empty apartment and felt an overwhelming sense of sadness mixed with love and contentment. She hadn't brought much with her to begin with, so packing had been easy. A few boxes and bags were lying scattered about the room, but that was it. She set off doing a deep clean to make sure she left the room sparkling, but since it was small and she was tidy, that didn't take long either. Now all she had to do was finish packing Jazzy's tack and gear…and say her goodbyes to Cooper. This would be their last night together.

They'd decided to have a quiet dinner at Cooper's house, so when Erin arrived that evening, she found him in the kitchen putting the final touches on the dish – corned beef and cabbage.

"I figured I couldn't let you go home without a classic Irish meal to remember me by," he said, his tone melancholy.

Cooper had already set the table with wine glasses and candles, trying to make this evening as special as possible. This was going to be a tough night.

They made light conversation throughout the meal – which was excellent, as usual – Cooper was a fantastic cook. But things were strained as neither of them wanted to address the elephant in the room. This was it, their last dinner together, their last night in each other's arms. By the time they had finished eating, Erin was almost in tears at the thought of not knowing when she'd see him again.

Sensing her fragile state, Cooper walked over to Erin, pulled her to her feet, and wrapped his arms around her. "It's okay, lass. Let's not think of goodbyes just yet. That's what tomorrow's for."

Erin nodded, dried her eyes, and grabbed Cooper's hand to lead him into the bedroom. This was their last night together, and she was going to make it count. She was overcome with a sense of urgency as the magnitude of this moment hit her.

She pulled off Cooper's shirt and unbuckled his pants while he tore at her clothes. In what felt like seconds, she was on the bed with him on top, and she grabbed at him and slid him inside. If this was it, their final night, she'd make it one to remember. It had to last until they saw each other again…and who knew when that would be.

When they both climaxed together, she cried out from the physical pleasure and the emotional pain. And then Erin's tears came, and Cooper held her as he fought back his own.

"Why does love hurt so much?" Erin asked. "Why does it have to be so hard?"

"It doesn't have to be. Just say the word, Erin. Say the word, and I'll be there. I'll wait for you for as long as it takes."

Chapter 35

Erin woke with a pit in her stomach. This was it, her last day. She'd pack her car, load her horse, and hit the road. Cooper would be leaving tomorrow, headed back across the pond with too many miles in between them for Erin to fathom.

But she'd think about all that later. Right now, there were horses to be fed and groomed and ridden. Ian had organized a farewell lunch for Erin and Cooper, and then Molly and her mother were scheduled to arrive around two o'clock that afternoon to help trailer Jazzy home.

And then it would all be over. Five beautiful, empowering, enlightening months – over.

She wouldn't dwell on it now though; she had horses to school, and Erin started with one last ride on Panther. After that it would be two of Ian's newer, green horses, and then Captain. She'd miss him so much too. He'd really developed under her training, and while Ian and Laney would take amazing care of him, of course, she knew he'd be unhappy. At least until he adjusted to life without Erin.

Erin took Panther to the outdoor and schooled over some fences. Then she spent the last portion of her ride out in the fields. She let the mare have a hair-raising, leg-stretching gallop in the lane at the very end of Ian's property, and Erin came back absolutely glowing. There was little that a good gallop couldn't fix.

Before she knew it, she was tacking up Cap for the last time and heading out into the ring. Ian came along to watch, and as his silence grew, Erin couldn't help but ask what he was thinking.

"How does he look?"

"Like a million bucks. The question is, will he ever go like that for anyone else?"

"I'm sure he will. He just has to find his next person. He or she is out there."

"Yeah, but it's definitely not me or Laney," he said with a dry laugh.

Still, despite her fears over Captain's abilities to perform for another rider, Erin finished up on a great note. She lavishly praised the horse as she brought him back inside for a quick rinse before heading back to his stall for the afternoon.

When Erin finished, she and Cooper were ushered into the tack room by Laney, and there they were met with some brightly colored balloons, streamers, and pizza. Ian and Paul were already inside slicing up the pizza pie and passing around some drinks. She sure was going to miss this place.

After everyone had had their fill of food, Ian stood up to make a toast.

"This is a sad day for Emerald Isle – we're losing two of the best staff members I've seen in a long time. Erin, you started here in January unsure of yourself, your place here at the farm, and your place in the world of eventing. But you worked your tail off, and you are certainly going places in the industry. I'm so proud to say that I've had a very, very small part to play in your continued success, and I'm excited to see the great things you do. However, if plans change course, you always have a home here. Thank you for all that you've done." The whole team clapped as Erin stood up to give Ian a big hug.

"Cooper, I always knew that your being here as my right-hand man was temporary, and I wish there was a way I could make you stay. Your contributions to the farm, the business, the horses, and the industry have been many, and I was always so proud to say, 'that's my cousin!' But I'd love you even if you weren't family because of your tremendous work ethic, positive attitude, and ability to train a horse to the very top. I honestly can't imagine what this team and farm will look like without you here," Ian paused for a moment as he looked like he was going to get emotional. "I don't think I'd be able to let you go if you were going anywhere else other than home to continue working with our family. You've become like a brother to me, and I'll never be able to thank you enough for everything you've done."

With that, the O'Ryans embraced, clapping each other on the back. Erin and Laney both had tears in their eyes as they watched the two cousins. They had been so inspirational for both of the girls, and they each counted themselves lucky to have worked alongside them.

"Before we go back to work, I do have a quick farewell present for Erin," Ian said as he looked at Cooper. "Coop, can you go grab it for me? I forgot to bring it in here."

"You didn't have to get me anything," Erin said. "You've already given me more than you'll ever know."

"Well, you deserve it. Think of it as a little something to remember us by." Ian smiled. "Okay, here's Coop. Let's go out into the aisle."

As Erin walked out of the tack room and rounded the corner, she gasped, and her hands flew up to her mouth. Cooper was standing there holding Captain – the horse was wearing a huge bright red ribbon tied around his neck.

"Are you serious?" Erin choked out.

Everyone was all smiles and laughing. "Yep. Coop and I decided the other day that we'd offer him to you. Captain loves you, and well, who are we to stand in the way of true love?" Ian had no idea how true his words were and that they made sense in more than one way in Erin's life.

Erin burst into tears as Laney came over and put her arm around her friend's shoulders.

"I know you're starting your own business, and another mouth to feed is probably the last thing you need," said Ian. "But he's yours if you want him."

Erin walked over and gave Ian another hug. "Yes, I'd love to have him. Thank you so much for everything." She then gave Cooper a hug, and he held her tightly. "Who are we to stand in the way of true love, right?" He whispered quietly so only she could hear.

Captain began to nuzzle Erin's shoulder, so she turned to him and gave his nose a kiss. "Looks like you're coming home with me, big guy." She stood there proudly holding her new horse as Laney snapped a few photos of them.

Erin's emotions were rolling around inside such that she felt as if she would explode. She was feeling so high and so low simultaneously that she didn't trust herself to speak for a bit. Tears silently fell down her cheeks as she again hugged each member of her team, saying goodbye for now, but not forever.

Chapter 36

The return trip home was uneventful, and Jazzy settled happily back into her old stall at Macy's. After unloading all of her tack, she let Jazzy out into the field with Hunter and Fitz, and the mare immediately returned to her old ways of bossing them around. It was good to see the gang back together.

Erin decided to take Captain to her parents' farm. Since that was where she would be basing her operation, she figured it would be best to take the gelding to settle in with the small herd that was there. After Erin moved into the carriage house at the beginning of July, she'd then move Jazzy to her parents' as well, so everyone would all be in one location.

Captain went out in the same field as Traveller and Ruby, their older retirees, and Gypsy, Molly's younger Thoroughbred. Cap, excited to meet his new friends, took off with Gypsy galloping around the field; Traveller and Ruby joined in for a brief lap or two, then, being older and wiser, went back to grazing. Cap and Gypsy continued with the silly antics for a little longer, then settled quietly and began grazing as well. So far, so good.

Erin was standing at the fence watching them for a bit longer to make sure everyone was getting along when Molly approached.

"A field full of Thoroughbreds – nothing makes me happier," Molly said with a smile. She was almost three and a half months pregnant, hardly showing, but she had her hand resting on her tiny belly anyway. "Well, that's not true. Having you home makes me happier."

"Aww sis," Erin said as she put an arm around her

Molly's shoulders. "You always did say the sweetest things," she laughed.

"It's true. We missed you. I know you weren't far, but you were so busy there was little time for visiting on either end. And now you're home and here to stay."

"That's the plan."

"Then why do I detect a note of sadness in your voice?"

Molly was the quiet one in the family, but she was also the most observant. There was little anyone could hide from her.

"Just sad that it's over, I guess. It's always bittersweet when a chapter ends and another begins, especially if the one you're leaving was so good."

"Well, at least you came home with a horse," Molly joked.

"It seems to be the thing to do, right? You returned home from Kentucky with Gypsy. Macy came home with Fitz. I had to keep up – I can't let you two outdo me!"

The girls laughed for a moment at the coincidence of it all. All three girls had acquired their horses rather suddenly, which isn't always the best way to get a horse. They are huge commitments, but in each of their cases, they couldn't leave them behind.

"Does Adam have any horses to send to you yet?"

"Yes, actually we talked earlier today on the drive home. He has two I can have as soon as I'm ready. Two geldings, both four years old, no limitations. They're still at Pimlico, but I'll probably pick them up day after tomorrow."

"Awesome, can't wait to meet them. New starts all around. You're back and running a business. Two racehorses are retiring and starting new careers. And I suppose Cooper takes off tomorrow to start his next chapter in Ireland. How are you feeling about that?"

"Like I screwed up."

"It's not too late to tell him to stay. He's already packed up and ready to go – just tell him to come here instead of back home."

"It's not that simple. I haven't known him that long. What if he's just a rebound and I end up being a waste of his time?"

"Beau and I didn't know each other that long before he quit his job in Kentucky and followed me back here."

"That's a good point. But you were in a better frame of mind then than I am now. You don't have a divorce hanging over your head."

"So what? And that divorce, in case you've forgotten, was finalized almost a year ago. It's time for you to move on. I know you feel guilty about everything, but it's time to let it go. As you know, Kevin's already engaged for goodness sake! He's put the past behind him – now you need to do the same."

"When did you get so smart?" Erin was always amazed at her sister's perception of life and everything in it. Molly could look at any situation and make sense of it so easily. No wonder she was such a gifted writer – she always knew how a story was going to end and how she was going to get there – a true problem solver.

"I learned everything I know from my big sister." She gave a wry smile.

"Get out of here!" Erin laughed. "Seriously though, thank you for this. You're right – I do have a lot of guilt about my failed marriage. But it's high time I let it go."

"So what are you going to do about Coop?"

"That, I still don't know. I don't want to ask him to give up his whole world and come to me – that doesn't seem fair. At least, I can't do anything like that until I'm sure."

"Sure of him?"

"No, sure of myself."

"I get it. And you'll get there – sooner than you think, too."

Chapter 37

The month of June unfolded and with it brought longer days, warm nights, and a very busy Erin. She brought her two new projects to the farm – two geldings named Nemo and Diego. They were both very green but willing and eager to please their new trainer. Erin's plan was to work with them steadily throughout the summer and then offer them for sale in the fall. She wouldn't rush it though – nothing would happen until she felt they were ready to move on.

By mid-June, Erin had packed most of her belongings at Macy's in preparation for her move down the street into the carriage house. It was located on another neighbor's farm and it only took her about five minutes to get to her mom's or Macy's. It was the perfect set up, and it felt like everything was falling into place.

"How are the new babies doing?" Macy asked one evening when she came home from work.

"They're both so good – I just love Thoroughbreds. They learn so quickly."

"Think you have time for another?"

"I believe so – why? Does Adam have another one coming off the track?"

"Yep, a filly. Sounds like she has a good brain."

"Any injuries?"

"Not that he mentioned. He's coming over tonight and said he'd talk to you about her."

"Nice! I think I could easily handle four or five in training at a time – in addition to Jazzy and Cap, of course."

"Will you keep Cap, or will you sell him at some point?"

"Nah, he's not going anywhere. He's family now. Besides, how could I sell a horse who adores me the way he does?" Erin had to admit that even though she loved Jazzy to death, Cap's obsession with her felt pretty nice. "I love that he picked me as his person."

"It's flattering, right?"

"Yes, that's a good word for it. Makes me feel like I'm doing something right," said Erin as she reached down to pet little Julep who was zooming around trying to get Erin's attention. But before she could lay her hands on the dog, the front doorbell rang, and Julep took off like a shot.

"Expecting anyone?" Erin asked.

"Just Adam, but not until later. And he comes through the back door." Macy made her way to the front of the house with Erin not far behind.

Standing there on the front porch was Leo. Dressed in grey slacks and a simple white button-up, it's clear he had come straight from work.

Julep, excited by the visitor and the prospect of belly rubs, began jumping up and down desperately trying to get Leo's attention.

"Hey Julep," he said as he bent down to pet the little dog. She immediately rolled over on her back, exposing her stomach for some scratches. Leo complied. "Sorry to drop by unannounced," he said looking up at Erin. "I was heading out to visit mom and had a few minutes to spare, and well, I saw on Facebook that you were back, so I thought I'd stop by and officially welcome you home." Erin, not one for social media, now remembered that Laney had tagged Erin in some farewell photos.

"It's no problem at all," Erin said, giving him a hug when he stood up. Julep, not satisfied with the amount of attention she was receiving, placed her paws against Leo's legs and began to bark.

"Okay, that's enough from you," Macy laughed as she picked up her dog. "Let me get this little peanut out of your hair. It's time for me to feed the horses anyway. Leo, it was good to see you again – sorry about my demanding pup."

"Yes, great to see you too. And no worries at all about Julep – she's very cute."

"That she is…this adorable little face saves her time and time again." With that, Macy turned and carried Julep outside to start their evening barn chores.

Erin led Leo into the kitchen at the back of the house. "Can I get you anything? Water, wine, coffee?"

"Oh no, I'm fine. Thank you. I just wanted to swing by, say hi, and see if you're free for dinner sometime soon." They both took seats at the table next to the windows that overlooked the back yard. Through them, they could see Julep bouncing along as Macy called to the horses to come in for their dinners.

Erin hesitated for a moment, but then plunged right in. "Leo, I would love to have dinner with you, but I'm not so sure that's a good idea. You see, I met someone while I was away, and even though we're not really officially together, it would just feel wrong to go out with you."

Leo's surprise briefly registered on his face, but he quickly caught himself. "It's no problem at all. I wasn't aware you had a boyfriend."

"I wouldn't say he's my boyfriend, but…well, it's complicated. He's currently in Ireland, and I'm here, but I wouldn't feel right doing dinner. At least, not right now."

"Ireland? Wow. That's some distance, but it's okay. I appreciate you being honest and letting me know."

"Of course. And if things change, well, I have

your number," she said with a smile. Even though she was falling in love with Cooper, Erin had to admit that Leo was handsome. And of course, there was always something to be said for someone you've known for years.

"Yes, please use it anytime."

As Leo got up to leave, Erin put a hand on his arm. "I do appreciate you stopping by. It's always good to see you…and if things were different, well, then of course I'd be interested in dinner. But my love life got a little tricky."

"It's okay, Erin. I really do understand. I just missed you, that's all," Leo said with a sad smile. "Your time away must have done you good though – you look great. Like you're in a really good place."

"I am. For the first time in years, I finally feel like I'm me again. Well, almost. But I'm a lot closer than I was before I left."

"I'm glad to hear it. Truly."

After Leo left, Erin made her way outside to help Macy with the rest of the barn chores. Macy had already fed the horses and was in the process of mucking stalls. Erin grabbed a pitchfork and got to work in Jazzy's stall.

"So? What was that about?" Macy asked.

"He asked me out to dinner. I told him that I was kind of seeing someone now, so it wouldn't feel right for me to accept his invitation."

"Really? It's just dinner. Maybe he just wanted to catch up."

"I don't think so – I just wouldn't feel right."

"But Cooper's in Ireland and you told me the other day that you didn't even know if you were officially together. No harm in keeping a spare around until you figure things out."

Erin started laughing so hard tears came to her eyes. "When did you start sounding so much like me? That sounds like advice I'd give."

"I guess I learned from the master. Go out and have fun – live a little!"

"Says the girl who's joined at the hip with her boyfriend!"

"Very true. But this is the way I see it. You're unsure about what to do with Cooper – and he's in Ireland anyway. Go out with Leo. Maybe being with him will help you make up your mind faster about Cooper. Like, being with Leo will solidify your love for Coop…or maybe you'll end up feeling the opposite."

"I get what you're saying, but I don't want to toy with Leo. That wouldn't be fair to him. Besides, I'm getting closer to figuring out what I want."

"Have you and Cooper been in touch?"

"We have. We text every day – and talk on the phone here and there. He's trying to give me time and space to figure out my next step."

"Which is?"

"Which is giving myself a little more time."

"How much time?"

"That, I don't know. But I don't want to rush anything – I want my next steps to be clear and each decision to be purposeful. I've rushed into a lot of things in my life, and sometimes they've worked out, but other times, they've blown up in my face. Before I ask Cooper to pack up and move here, I want to be completely sure of myself and what I want." Erin paused for a moment to move the wheelbarrow over to Fitz's stall. "But I will say, I'm leaning towards asking him to come here. But timing is everything – and I want to make sure what I'm feeling now is real. Does that make sense?"

"It does. You want to be with him now because you just left him not long ago. Of course you miss him like crazy. But you're wondering if absence will make the heart grow fonder, right?"

"Exactly. Will I miss him more as time goes on…or less? And until I know that, I can't ask him to uproot his whole life for me."

"I understand. But you also have to remember that nothing's permanent. If you ask him to come here and things don't work out, that's okay. He can pack up and go home – or back to Ian's. And that wouldn't be your fault. Sometimes relationships just don't work out – even when they seemed rock solid in the beginning." Macy was realizing that Erin's hesitancy to take the leap with Cooper all stemmed from her broken marriage.

"I know, and you're right, but I just don't want to turn someone else's life upside down. I threw Kevin a curveball he wasn't expecting, and it destroyed us."

"I know, but history doesn't always repeat itself. Just because your marriage didn't last doesn't mean you're not capable of having a lasting relationship with someone else."

"You're right…but still, I just need more time."

"Then take it. But stop beating yourself up about Kevin. What happened is over and done with. You've both moved on, and I'd say you're both happier for it."

"I agree – I think we're both heading down the right paths. But still, I just want to play it safe."

"Of course you do. And you'll figure it all out in time. One day you'll wake up and you'll just know what to do."

"I hope so," Erin smiled at her friend. "You ever notice how easy it is to solve all of life's problems while mucking stalls?"

Macy laughed because it was so true.

Chapter 38

The summer flew by. Erin spent her days in riding tights, tank tops, and running between her parents' and Macy's farms. She'd decided to leave Jazzy at Macy's for the time-being since the mare was so well-adjusted there and also because it was a great excuse to see her friend and catch up with one another at the end of a long day.

While Erin's routine varied day by day, she typically spent her mornings working on her project horses and her evenings riding with Macy after the sun had started to set and Macy was home from work. At one point in late July, Erin had four horses in training, Jazzy and Captain not included. But one had already sold to a nearby foxhunter, and Erin was thrilled that the filly would be close, and she could check up on her from time to time.

In order to help make ends meet, financially, Erin had also started working for Beau. He'd hired a secretary months ago, but she was semi-retired, and was only really looking for part-time work. She chose Mondays, Wednesdays, and Fridays, and Erin filled in on Tuesdays and Thursdays. Erin arrived late morning, typically, after she'd taken care of and ridden most, if not all, of her horses. Then she worked well into the evening until it was time to head back to the barn for the nightly chores.

She'd never been busier in her life, but Erin was enjoying every second of this new chapter.

On weekends she ventured to local horse shows, alternating between larger scale events for Jazzy and Captain, who were now charging around cross country like they'd done it their whole lives, and smaller, low key shows for her projects. Having show experience was very helpful in setting these horses up for their new careers. It also helped Erin figure out the direction they should head, be it hunters, jumpers, eventing, etc. The most important thing was giving these horses an education. A well-trained horse usually ended up in good hands, and Erin did everything she could to arm her new charges with the tools they'd need to succeed.

The hardest part, of course, was saying goodbye when they sold. Erin tried to keep a distance, as much as possible anyway, with the sale horses knowing that they'd be moving on, but it was tough. When the sweet little filly sold, even though Erin knew her new owner well, it still didn't stop her from crying her eyes out as the trailer pulled away.

Erin vowed to keep in touch with the owners of her horses and would also promise to take horses back if they weren't a perfect match with their new life. It was important to her that her "kids," as she'd started calling them, ended up in good, safe places, and if that meant taking one back to save it from a potentially dangerous situation, then so be it.

In the midst of all the riding, working, and crisscrossing the town of Monkton as she drove from farm to farm, Erin moved out of Macy's into the carriage house Molly had rented years ago. The house was small, but clean and well-appointed with one bedroom, one bathroom, an office, and a large eat-in kitchen. Erin loved it. She'd always adored it when Molly lived there, and now it just felt right that she was calling it her home as well. At the end of every long day, Erin looked forward to returning to her humble little abode.

It was dusk by the time Erin pulled into the driveway of her house, and she was surprised to see Molly's SUV parked out front. Erin found Molly sitting in one of the chairs on the back porch that overlooked the expanse of grassy fields beyond.

"I always loved ending my days out here where everything was so peaceful and quiet, watching the world tuck itself in for the night," Molly said as Erin approached.

Now that it was late August, Molly was more than five months pregnant and even though she was showing, her belly was still tiny. She and Beau could have found out the gender by now, but both had decided they wanted to wait until the baby was born and be surprised. Erin and Macy, both planners, wanted to start buying all the baby clothes and items – either pink or blue – but Molly was adamant. They'd find out in just a few more short months.

"I usually grab something quick to eat and sit out here until the lightning bugs come out."

"Sorry to drop by unexpectedly. Beau had an emergency, and I just felt restless. I also wanted to see if you'd heard about Kevin."

"What about him?" Erin had heard he and Delaney had gotten married earlier in the summer. He certainly wasted no time.

"They're pregnant."

Wow – he really didn't waste time. "How do you know?"

"I saw her in the maternity section of Nordstrom today. She doesn't know who I am, of course, but I recognized her from Kevin's pictures on social media. She's not really showing yet, so I wasn't completely sure, but then I heard her tell the clerk that she's eight weeks. They made a honeymoon baby, supposedly."

Erin remained silent, attempting to sort through the thoughts whirling around in her head.

"What are you thinking?" Molly asked.

"Honestly? My first thought is better her than

me." That, right then, was how Erin knew that she was over him. Over their marriage and over the last crazy few years. "Truly. I wish him nothing but happiness. I do. And it sounds like he's getting everything he wants."

"What about you? You're happy, right?" Molly so desperately worried about her sister, out on her own now, carving a new path through life. If anyone could do it, Erin could, but like any loving sister, Molly just worried.

Erin's smile was genuine. "So happy. I've still got a lot of figure out, and I have no idea where this next bend in the road will take me, but I'm looking forward to seeing where it all goes."

"No regrets then?"

"None. And actually, I have a plan for me and Cooper. One that allows us to move forward but still play it a little safe at the same time."

The two sisters caught up for a while, and after Molly left, Erin went inside to make a quick dinner of scrambled eggs and toast.

Thoughts of Cooper had been laying heavily on her heart recently, and now, emboldened and encouraged by Kevin's ability to go after what he wanted, Erin decided that the time had come. You only lived one life – it was your responsibility to go after what you wanted.

She realized it was in the middle of the night in Ireland, but she didn't care. Erin pulled up Cooper's number on her phone and pushed send. *Here goes nothing.*

"Lass?" Cooper answered, voice thick and groggy with sleep. "Everything okay?"

Erin smiled at the sound of his voice. "Yes, my love, everything's wonderful."

Cooper paused for a moment. "Are you calling to

say the word?" That had been his line. *Just say the word, and I'm there.*

"Not exactly. Not yet anyway. I was calling to ask if I could come visit for a bit. Maybe a week or two? I figured before I said the word, before I asked you to move your life halfway around the world, it might be wise to make sure we still like each other."

"Oh lass, I don't think we need to worry about that," he laughed.

"I know. But just for me – for my peace of mind – let me come to you. And if we still get along alright, then I'll say the word. Deal?"

"Deal." She could hear his smile through the phone. "Lass?"

"Yeah?"

"I love you."

"I love you too." She'd finally said it.

WHAT'S NEW?

Stay tuned for Laurie's upcoming short story collection, *Country Mouse & Other Stories*, to be published this Winter season! This collection will feature a variety of stories including a stand-alone piece on Cassidy Winters, (a previous character from *Where the Bluegrass Grows* and *Kicking On*), as well as "Basket Case," which is the start of an all-new young adult series!

Also, look for Book 4 of the *Equestrian Romance Series* which will feature Erin's upcoming Irish adventure!

~ Acknowledgements ~

I can't believe I started *and finished* a book in one whole year – a record for me! Let's hope I can keep it up!

To my readers – I couldn't do this without you. The emails, the messages on social media, the comments on my Instagram posts – each and every one encourages me to sit down, write, and create a new equestrian world for all of you. I appreciate every piece of feedback I receive – you guys are the best, and I can't thank you enough!

To my Instagram followers – thank you for sending horse name suggestions when I was feeling a little stuck. A few of them made it into this book – look for the ones that didn't to be featured in upcoming titles!

To some of my #1 fans – my family – Kay Yeager, Kim Gerhardt, and Sylvia Berglie – love you!

And James – I did it – another one! Thank you for helping with my website and marketing materials and for being the best support system 24/7. You are always willing to talk shop, and I love you so much.

~ About the Author ~

Laurie Berglie lives in Maryland with her husband, James, and their 8 four-legged kids. She enjoys renovating her fixer-upper farm, reading horse books, and competing in the hunters. She has a BA in English from Stevenson University and an MA in Humanities from Towson University.

For more information, please visit: www.laurieberglie.com or her blog at www.themarylandequestrian.com. You can also find her on Instagram @marylandequestrian.

If you liked this book, please consider writing a short review on Amazon or Goodreads! They help so much and mean the world to us self-published authors! Thank you!

Made in the USA
Monee, IL
29 January 2021